Ophelia Amaru
Your Soul is sacred

Ophelia Amaru

Your Soul is Sacred

A collection of words for healing & wholeness

Spirituality | Self-help | Poetry

Bibliografische Information der Deutschen Nationalbibliothek: Die Deutsche Nationalbibliothek verzeichnet diese Publikation in der Deutschen Nationalbibliografie; detaillierte bibliografische Daten sind im Internet über http://dnb.dnb.de abrufbar.

Die automatisierte Analyse des Werkes, um daraus Informationen insbesondere über Muster, Trends und Korrelationen gemäß §44b UrhG („Text und Data Mining") zu gewinnen, ist untersagt.

© 2025 Ophelia Amaru

Verlag: BoD · Books on Demand GmbH, In de Tarpen 42, 22848 Norderstedt, bod@bod.de

Druck: Libri Plureos GmbH, Friedensallee 273, 22763 Hamburg

ISBN: 978-3-7693-7761-3

WELCOME HOME, DEAR SOUL

A Celestial Reminder 12

A Sacred Welcome 17

A Living prayer 30

INVOCATION 38

WHISPERS OF THE SHADOWS 42

A Message from Pluto 47

In the darkness 50

Finding Wholeness in the Darkness 51

Cocooning Darkness 60

Surrender into the Darkness 61

Shadowy Mountains 70

The Wild Within 71

Waves of Emotions 79

The Ocean within 82

DIVINE CONNECTIONS 90

A message from Wiraqocha 95

Luring Whispers 99

Awakening the Magic Within 100

A Soul's Prayer 109

Embracing The Divine Connection 112

Child of the Universe 122

Birthed by the Stars Cosmic DNA 124

Devotion 135

Devotion a Path to Grace 138

Goddess of the Universe 150

The Cosmic Dance of Love and Grace 151

EMBRACING THE SELF 160

Message from Aphrodite	165
Dance with Emotions	169
Emotional Dance	172
She	184
Radical Self-acceptance	185
Lurking Fire	195
Ignite the Fire Within	196
Madness	206
Finding Home Through Madness	207
RAYS OF LIGHT	216
A Message from Ch'aska	220
Beneath all my layers	224
Unveiling the Light Within	225
Reclaiming Humaness	234
Being Human	235
You are enough	244
Your Divine Essence	246
Emotional Safety	256
Trusting the Sanctuary Within	258
CYCLE & SEASONS	268
A Message from Gaia and Luna	271
I am the Seasons	275
Embracing the Seasons Within	277
Unfolding	286
Unfolding into Wholeness	287
Nature's Daughter	296
The Wild Within Connection and Belonging	298
Nectar of Life	308
Savor the Nectar of Life	310

GRATITUDE	319
ABOUT THE AUTHOR	321
SOUL CONNECTION	323
MY GIFT FOR YOU	326
OFFERINGS	327

With Love for the Earth

As you hold this book, I want you to know that it is more than a collection of words—it is a living prayer of reciprocity. **One tree will be planted for every copy sold**, breathing life back into our sacred Mother Earth. This act of giving is rooted in the Andean concept of *aini*, the sacred principle of reciprocity.

It is my way of honoring the balance between receiving and giving, and together, we can nourish the earth that holds us so tenderly.

Ps.: no matter if you're reading the digital or printed version, a tree will be planted for **every** copy.

A CELESTIAL REMINDER

My love, take a moment to gaze at your wrist. See the delicate blue veins weaving just beneath your skin, like rivers carrying life through your body. What flows within you is more than blood—it is the essence of the universe itself.

The hemoglobin in your veins, the iron that fuels your life, was born in the fiery heart of a dying star. Yes, darling, you are built from stardust—ancient fragments of cosmic fire, forged in the crucible of creation and carried across time to become you.

Every breath you take, every beat of your heart, is powered by the universe that birthed galaxies, lit up the night sky, and whispered its magic into existence. You are not separate from this vast cosmos. You are it.

Imagine the stars that shimmer in the velvet darkness above, and know this: they sing the same eternal song as your soul. The great galaxies spiraling through the void, the constellations mapped across eternity—they reflect the dance of your very atoms, moving in harmony with the infinite.

Even the chaos of the cosmos—the meteors that burn and collide, the black holes that pull everything inward—speaks to the beauty of your human experience. The messy moments, the stumbles, and the heartaches are not failures. They are your creation. They are the proof that you, too, hold the vastness of the universe within you.

So, when the weight of the world feels heavy, when doubt whispers that you are not enough, remember this truth:

You are stardust-given form—a radiant being carrying the light of the stars within your very veins.

May this knowing anchor you, my love, and remind you that even in the wildest storms, the universe flows through you, guiding you home to yourself. Always.

You are infinite

You are eternal

A SACRED WELCOME

Welcome, dear soul,

I'm overly grateful that you've picked up this book and are about to embark on a deeply transformative journey with me.

YOU SOUL IS SACRED is more than just a collection of poems and prayers; it's an offering of love, a warm embrace, a safe space where you can rest, reflect, to reconnect with yourself and the divinity within you. Consider this book a sacred companion—a best friend in written form—here to offer you comfort, guidance, and a gentle hand to hold as you journey through life's cycles of light and darkness.

Within these pages, you'll find reflections of my soul in the form of poetry, prayers, and essays. Each piece was created to nurture your inner world, helping you find the quiet strength that lies deep within you. As you move through the chapters, you'll notice there's a space for every emotion—a place for joy, grief, gratitude, and growth. My intention is, that this book feels like a soft, comforting blanket wrapped around you, reminding you that you are held, seen, and loved in all your seasons.

Each poem is paired with an essay that explores the space between the words, diving deeper into the themes of healing, transformation, and divine connection. These essays offer insights into the poems and prayers while standing on their own as reflections of the energies we encounter on the journey to wholeness.

How to Use This Book

This is not a book to be read quickly or consumed in one sitting. Instead, I invite you to approach it with intention and openness. Perhaps you'll choose to read one poem a day, allowing the words to sink into your soul before moving on. Or maybe you'll feel called to open the book at random, trusting that the message you land on is exactly what you need in that moment. Trust your intuition—it will guide you.

The essays offer you an opportunity to reflect more deeply on the themes at hand. They can serve as companions to the poems or as stand-alone musings to explore at your own pace. You'll also notice that each essay is followed by gentle reflection questions or journal prompts. These are invitations to take the experience a step further—an encouragement to pause, to listen even deeper, and to engage with the whispers of your soul.

The lined pages following the prompts are here for you to journal your thoughts, emotions, and insights as they arise. Consider these pages a soft nudge to tune into your inner world. What comes up for you as you reflect? What emotions stir as you read? What truths or insights are ready to be written down? Let this book become a space for your self-discovery.

These journal prompts are not meant to be tasks or assignments, but gentle companions on your journey. There is no rush, no pressure. Use the pages to express yourself freely—whether that means writing down your thoughts, doodling, or simply letting your pen wander. This book is here to meet you exactly where you are and hold space for whatever arises.

As you journal, you may find yourself returning to certain poems, essays, or questions—trust that instinct. Every word in this book is a gateway to deeper healing, and the prompts are here to guide you along that path. You may also come across blank pages—gentle pauses woven into the rhythm of this book. These pages are yours to fill with whatever speaks to your heart: doodles, words, pressed flowers, or even a treasured photograph. Or perhaps, leave them untouched—a quiet sanctuary, a space for your soul to breathe and simply be. These blank pages, like the spaces within you, are sacred.

Honoring Mama Moon

Mama Moon has always held a sacred place in my heart. She was the first energy I prayed to when my world felt like it was crumbling. In her quiet glow, I found solace; in her phases, I found guidance. Her gentle yet powerful presence reminded me of the beauty in impermanence, that nothing is static, and all things—emotions, experiences, and phases of life—are meant to flow and change.

As a priestess, I work deeply with the energy of the moon, honoring her cycles as a reflection of our own. She teaches us that every phase is beautiful in its own way—the darkness of the New Moon holds the promise of new beginnings, the growing light of the Waxing Crescent mirrors the energy of intention and expansion, and the radiant Full Moon reminds us to celebrate and shine. The quiet surrender of the Waning Crescent teaches the art of letting go, while the First Quarter, with its balance of light and shadow, calls us to take action and embrace ourselves fully.

In creating this book, it felt only natural to align its sections with the phases of Mama Moon. Each phase carries an energy that flows through the chapters, mirroring the themes and wisdom they hold.

Whispers of Shadows is connected to the **New Moon**, a time of introspection and planting seeds in the fertile soil of darkness. This section explores the shadowy whispers of our soul and the beginnings of transformation.

Divine Connections aligns with the **Waxing Crescent**, representing the growing light and the call to deepen our connection with the divine, as intentions begin to take shape.

Embracing the Self reflects the **First Quarter Moon**, a phase of strength and balance, where we take inspired action and face the challenges that come with loving and accepting ourselves fully.

Rays of Light shines brightly with the energy of the **Full Moon**, symbolizing illumination, celebration, and the radiant joy of stepping into our light.

Cycle and Season flows with the **Waning Crescent**, a phase of surrender, reflection, and honoring the endings that make space for new beginnings.

By aligning the sections of this book with the moon's phases, I want to honor her teachings and invite you to flow with her rhythm as you move through these pages. May her light guide you as it has guided me, and may you find beauty in every phase of your journey—just as she has shown me.

And as you journey through this book, I invite you to carry Mama Moon's wisdom with you. The next time you gaze up at her glowing face, remember that you are not alone.

You are looking at the same moon that your ancestors once gazed upon, the same moon that witnessed their prayers, their dances, their whispers to the divine.

Through her light, we are connected—across time, space, and lifetimes. The lineage of all that your soul has ever been, and all that it will become, is woven into her cycles. Every prayer you speak, every intention you set, every moment you pause under her glow, you honor this sacred connection.

Let Mama Moon be your guide, just as she has been for countless souls before you. She reminds us that we are part of something eternal, a dance of light and shadow, of beginnings and endings, held within her embrace.

My Intention

When I created this book, I did so with the heartfelt intention of offering you a space for healing, transformation, and reconnection. The poems and prayers found here are born from my own journey—moments of joy, sorrow, deep reflection, and spiritual awakening. They are the result of countless nights where the words came pouring out, urging to be expressed.

In this book, when I speak of the divine, of prayer, or wholeness, know that I do so not in the context of any particular religious tradition, but from a place of universal reverence. The divine, to me, is the life force that connects us all—the energy that flows through us and around us, the essence of love, light, and everything in between.

These poems and prayers are my sacred devotion, my way of communing with the universe, and I offer them to you with the hope that they will resonate in your heart as well.

A Sacred Invitation

Take this book in your hands, feel its weight, and know that it holds space for your soul to breathe. I encourage you to sit with it in moments of stillness. Light a candle, brew your favorite tea or ceremonial cacao, and let the words work their magic. Whether you use it as an oracle, opening to a random page, or as a daily practice, reading one poem or essay at a time—know that there is no right or wrong way to engage with these pages.

As you journey through, let yourself feel everything. Let yourself be both the seeker and the found. This book is your sanctuary, a place to meet yourself with love, kindness, and acceptance.

I believe in the power of words to heal, to uplift, and to transform. I believe in the magic that happens when we listen to the whispers within, and my deepest hope is that you will find that magic here too. You are never alone on this path. Wherever you are right now, you are exactly where you need to be. Trust in that. Trust in yourself. Allow the words to guide you back to the truth of who you are—whole, radiant, and deeply loved.

May this book feel like a melting hug for your soul.

With all my love and blessings,

Ophelia Amaru

P.S. Just like you and I, this book does not strive for perfection. As a self-published author, I consciously chose not to have it professionally proofread, embracing the rawness of its creation. It is as imperfectly perfect as the journey of life itself.

Inhale

Exhale

A LIVING PRAYER

I didn't always know the power of prayer. For a long time, the word felt distant to me, tethered to the confines of religion and ceremony, something I didn't fully resonate with. But then, life brought me to a turning point—a moment when everything felt shattered. My world was crumbling, and I was lost, helpless, and dependent in ways that felt unbearable. In the silence of those days, when loneliness wrapped itself around me like a heavy cloak, I turned to prayer.

At first, I prayed softly, almost hesitantly, whispering into the stillness so I wouldn't be overheard. I prayed to Mother Earth, asking her to take the weight of my burdens. I prayed to the universe, pleading for direction and for a spirit to guide and steady me. I prayed to Mama Moon, seeking her wisdom to embrace all of my phases and emotions, and to teach me the infinite beauty in impermanence.

Then, as if guided by something deep and ancient, I found myself drawn to Wiraqocha, the Great Creator of Andean mythology. A bond began to form—a knowing that I was heard. I started learning words in Quechua, the sacred language of the Andes, letting the sound of these prayers flow from my soul. They were small steps at first, tentative and unfamiliar, yet they felt deeply right as if I were answering a call I had always known.

I prayed every day, not with perfect words or elaborate rituals, but with my heart wide open. Each prayer became a bridge, connecting me to something greater, something unseen yet deeply felt. I prayed when I needed guidance, when I longed for reassurance, and when I sought the nurturing embrace of Mother Earth.

Through this journey, I began to see prayer in a new light. What I once thought belonged to churches and rituals became something far more intimate and expansive. I realized that "God" does not have to fit a single image or belief.

God can be anything—a flower, the wind, the sun, or even ourselves.

Prayer is not about the "who" or "what" we pray to; it is about the intention behind it, the offering of our truth in its purest form.

And then, the blessings began to flow. Within a week, I reclaimed my independence, taking steps I didn't think I was brave enough to take. I trusted the whispers of spirit and followed where they led me. What I received in return was beyond anything I could have imagined.

But I've come to understand that blessings do not always arrive in the form we expect. Sometimes, they come cloaked in challenges, burdens, or pain. They shake us, strip away what no longer serves, or bring us face-to-face with our deepest fears. These moments—while shattering at the time—often hold the greatest gifts. They are blessings in disguise, their true nature revealed only after the storm has calmed.

I've lived this truth. In one moment, I found myself standing before my darkest shadows, humiliated and ashamed. It felt as though the ground had been pulled from beneath me, leaving me exposed and broken. At the time, it seemed like anything but a blessing. Yet, with time came wisdom. That moment, as painful as it was, became my turning point. It shattered the illusions I had clung to and forced me to vow to myself—to reclaim my sovereignty, to change my direction, to rise again.

Not all blessings come with such trials. Some arrive in their fullness, far exceeding what we prayed for. They may even feel overwhelming, unfamiliar, or too abundant to accept. Divine blessings are pure, and given without expectation, obligation, or demand. They are gifts from a source that asks for nothing in return but gratitude.

And so, I learned to give thanks—for every blessing, whether it arrived wrapped in light or shadow. For even in the moments when I felt most broken,

I was being held, guided, and transformed by a force greater than myself.

Gratitude poured from me in tears—tears of relief, of joy, and of a heart overflowing with the knowing that I was cradled tenderly yet powerfully by the divine. Every prayer I had spoken, every whispered plea, had been heard. What I received in return was far greater than I could have imagined.

I remember as it was yesterday, the moment when my new - my OWN - laptop arrived. I sat there, in my cozy seat, wrapped in blankets. I cradled the box with that laptop like it was a child, I simply held it, close to my heart. And I cried. I cried tears of relief, of gratitude and pride. I let them pour out of me, a deep allowing to feel, to really feel the abundance and blessings. It took around an hour before I finally unboxed it.

Be grateful, always. For the obvious blessings, for the ones that arrive disguised as challenges, and for those that stretch your capacity to receive. Each carries a gift, a lesson, a transformation waiting to unfold.

This shift was liberating. Suddenly, prayer felt alive, limitless, and deeply personal. It became a way to connect with the world around me and within me. A prayer could be as simple as standing barefoot on the earth, feeling her pulse beneath my feet, or as quiet as a breath whispered into the morning air. It could be the way I nourished myself with a lovingly prepared meal, the stillness I found in a cup of cacao, or the words I spoke with care and intention.

> ***Prayer is not confined to sacred places;***
> ***it is the sacred place.***

It is the energy we offer, the connection we seek, and the trust we place in the unseen. And when we pray from this space, with hearts wide open, we align ourselves with something far greater—a rhythm, a force, a love that holds us tenderly yet powerfully.

This is what I discovered: prayer is not just about asking; it is about being. It is an act of courage, of surrender, and trust. It is our way of saying,

"I am here, I am listening, and I am ready to receive." And in that readiness, miracles unfold.

Whether you pray to a star, a stone, or the divine spark within yourself, it does not matter. What matters is the intention, the openness, and the truth that it is yours.

In prayer, we find not just answers but a homecoming—a return to the sacred essence of who we are.

Let this chapter, and this book, be an invitation to create your own living prayer. To nourish your soul with words, gestures, and moments that feel true to you. To embrace the limitless beauty of prayer, knowing that every whispered intention is heard and held.

Invoking the Sacred

Before you dive into these pages, I invite you to pause, breathe deeply, and take a moment to honor your journey. The invocation you will find on the next pages is not merely a collection of words

—it is a portal, a sacred call to align with the divine energies that surround you. Let these words hold you, like the most tender embrace, as you set your intentions for this journey.

Feel free to read it aloud, or simply close your eyes and let its essence flow through you. Each time you return to it, you weave a deeper connection to yourself and the infinite love that holds you. Let this be your reminder: **you are seen, you are safe, and you are always held in divine grace.**

INVOCATION

*Divine Source of all creation,
infinite and boundless in love,
I gather here within this sacred space,
my heart open, my spirit aligned,
ready to weave the threads of this journey.*

*As I step into the depths of my soul,
I call upon your presence, your guidance,
to illuminate my path with clarity
and nurture my growth with tender care.*

*Bless these words that flow onto these pages—
each poem, each prayer, a spark of the divine.
May they become rays of light,
tendrils of starlight,
guiding me home to myself.*

*Grant me the courage to embrace
the fullness of my humanity,
to honor the shadows as much as the light,
and to see the sacred beauty in every moment,
and within myself.*

*May this creation become a sanctuary,
a refuge of solace and inspiration,
a place where the soul finds its home,
and the heart is cradled by grace.*

*As above so below
as within so without
And so it is.*

WHISPERS OF THE SHADOWS

There are moments in life when the shadows feel closer than the light, cloaking us in their quiet embrace and whispering truths we've long buried within. These whispers often echo with fear, sorrow, or fragments of ourselves we've hidden away—parts that feel too heavy to hold or too raw to face. Yet, these shadows are not our adversaries. They are the sacred messengers of the soul, guiding us gently toward the hidden depths of our being.

To walk through the valley of our own shadows is not an act of defeat but of courage. It is an invitation to enter a sacred space within—a place where the parts of ourselves we've neglected or silenced wait patiently, yearning to be seen, heard, and embraced with tenderness. In the quiet of these moments, we are called to sit with our shadows, not to banish them, but to honor them as integral threads in the tapestry of who we are.

A Sacred Invitation to Love Your Shadows

This chapter invites you to step into the sanctuary of your inner world, where shadows weave their quiet symphony. It is not a call to confront or conquer, but to meet these parts of yourself with an open heart. As you turn these pages, may you find the courage to pause and listen to the whispers within—those subtle nudges that guide you toward a deeper understanding of your own soul.

In this journey, you will find that the shadows are not here to harm you but to guide you. They hold within them the lessons you've long sought, the truths you've been too weary to face. As you walk through their gentle embrace, you may discover that even the heaviest darkness carries the seeds of light, waiting to bloom in the soil of your acceptance.

The Light Within the Darkness

The shadows remind us that growth often begins in unseen places. Just as seeds sprout in the quiet depths of the earth, so too does our healing begin in the stillness of the unknown. It is in this sacred space of reflection and surrender that we find the light woven into the darkness, revealing the beauty of our own becoming.

This chapter is a love letter to your resilience, your courage, and your infinite capacity to hold space for yourself. Within these words lies an invitation to dance with the shadows, to see them not as burdens but as companions on your journey. For within their depths lies a profound truth: that you are whole, even in the places you've yet to embrace.

Embracing All That You Are

As you embark on this tender exploration, know that every shadow you meet holds a gift. It is an opportunity to reclaim the parts of yourself you've forgotten, to love the parts you've rejected, and to remember the strength that lies in your vulnerability. In walking through this valley, you are not only rediscovering your own light but learning to carry it with grace into even the darkest corners of your soul.

Let these pages be a mirror, reflecting both your shadows and your stars. May they remind you that within every whisper of darkness, there is a song of light—a song that only you can sing. As you move through this chapter, may you feel held, seen, and loved by the infinite wisdom that resides within you.

Take a deep breath, dear soul. Step into this space with trust, knowing that you are safe to explore, to feel, and to be. The shadows are not here to harm you; they are here to guide you home to yourself.

As I'm working deeply with the cosmic energies, I channeled a message from Pluto, in astrology, he is known for his soul-stirring and deep transformational energy and shadow work. For me, he's the Lord of my Shadows. And I'm humbled to share the message I received from him and be the vessel for the wisdom it carries.

Dance in the dark,
my Dear, dance

A MESSAGE FROM PLUTO

Welcome, brave soul.

You stand at the threshold of your own shadow, the place where truths lie hidden and fears whisper their stories. Do not fear the darkness—it is not your enemy but your teacher, your guide, the keeper of all you've buried and forgotten.

In the shadows, you will find the fragments of yourself you thought were lost, the raw, unpolished truths that shape who you are. These whispers are not here to break you but to awaken you. They call you to shed the masks you wear, to release the burdens you carry, and to claim the light you've always held within. Transformation is not a gentle thing; it is a fire that burns away what no longer serves. But you, brave soul, are not here to be consumed—you are here to rise from the ashes, whole and radiant.

Step forward with courage. I will be here, steady in the shadows, watching as you uncover the beauty of your depths and become the light you were always meant to be.

- Pluto, Lord of the Shadows

IN THE DARKNESS

In the darkness
She reveals her shadows
Facing her deepest fears
Screams for her highest prayers

In the darkness
She sees the stars
with her naked soul

In the darkness
She is whole

FINDING WHOLENESS IN THE DARKNESS

The Beauty Within Darkness

Caught in the hustle and bustle of our lives, we often find ourselves seeking the light—the brightness that illuminates our path and guides us through the darkest of nights. We yearn for clarity, for certainty, for a sense of security in a world that can often feel chaotic and uncertain.

But what if I told you that there is beauty to be found in the darkness? What if I told you that within the velvety darkness of your being resides a treasure trove of wisdom, resilience, and untapped strength, waiting for your embrace, to be discovered and opened?

Darkness is not a villain we have to fight against; it is a sanctuary, a sacred space where your soul can breathe, unravel, and rest—where even the shadows long for our unconditional love.

It is here, in the quiet embrace of the unknown, that transformation begins.

I invite you to journey into the depths of your own darkness with courage and grace. Of course, it will challenge you to confront your deepest fears and insecurities. Remember about the knowing that they hold the keys to your greatest truths and strengths.

The Transformative Power of Shadows

Embracing the darkness within ourselves is an unwavering transformative power. I remind you that it is only by seeing your shadow's face - to face, that when you truly experience healing and wholeness. It is in the darkness that we find the space to unravel, to explore, to grow—to become the fullest expression of ourselves.

In a culture that often shuns vulnerability and celebrates only the bright and shiny aspects of life, "Good vibes only", it can be easy to overlook the profound beauty and wisdom that resides in the shadows. Let yourself be reminded, that it is precisely in the darkness that we discover the source of resilience, courage, and authenticity.

Surrendering to the Depths

So how do we embrace the darkness within ourselves? How do we find the courage to confront our deepest fears and insecurities?

The answer lies in surrender—in allowing ourselves to be fully present with whatever arises, without judgment or resistance. It lies in cultivating a sense of compassion and self-love that extends to even the darkest corners of our being. It lies in recognizing that the darkness is not something to be feared or avoided, but something to be embraced and explored.

Through practices such as meditation, journaling, and self-reflection, we can begin to shine a light into the depths of our own darkness. We can begin to unearth the hidden gems that lie buried beneath the surface, waiting to be discovered.

Finding Wholeness in the Dark

And as we journey deeper into the darkness, we come to realize that it is not something to be overcome or conquered, but something to be honored, yet to be worshipped and celebrated. For it is in the darkness that we find the courage to face our fears, to confront our shadows, and to emerge stronger, wiser, and more whole than ever before.

So let us embrace the depths of our own being, my loves. Let us journey into the darkness with open hearts and open minds, knowing that it is only by fully embracing all aspects of ourselves that we can truly experience the beauty and richness of life.

And in the darkness, may we find not only our shadows but also our own sky full of stars—the guiding lights that illuminate our path and remind us of the infinite potential that resides within us all.

Think of a time when you faced your deepest fears and emerged stronger. How did it feel to confront and grow through that experience?

How can you create space in your life to honor the darkness within you as a sacred opportunity for healing and transformation?

What would it feel like to see your shadows as companions rather than villains?

In the darkness,
we are whole.

COCOONING DARKNESS

When the darkness spread its mighty wings

I let them cocoon me

Pouring over me like a gentle velvety kiss

I let the darkness carry me away

Cocooning me softly

Gentle touching every inch of my soul

I surrender to be reminded

That sparkling stars

are only to be seen in the darkness

SURRENDER INTO THE DARKNESS

An Invitation to Rest in the Shadows

In our lives, darkness often carries a misunderstood reputation—one of fear, avoidance, and discomfort. Yet, within its velvety embrace lies a profound potential for transformation and solace. Darkness is not simply an absence of light; it is a sanctuary, a place where the soul can rest and reflect, free from the piercing gaze of the external world. It is the sacred cocoon that gently envelops us, inviting us to surrender and listen to the whispers of our inner being.

To step into the darkness is to embrace the natural cycles of existence—the ebbs and flows, the light and the shadow, the seen and the unseen. It is a quiet reminder that not all growth is visible. Just as the moon waxes and wanes, and the stars find their brilliance in the night sky, our journeys, too, require moments of retreat and reflection. Darkness becomes the fertile ground where the seeds of our deepest truths are sown, nurtured by the silence and the quiet touch of the unknown.

The Beauty of the Cocoon

When we allow ourselves to be cocooned by the darkness, it is an act of trust and surrender. We release the need to control, to constantly seek the light, and instead, we allow the darkness to cradle us in its gentle arms. In this space, we find the courage to face our shadows—not as adversaries, but as guides illuminating the parts of ourselves we may have hidden away. Each shadow carries a gift, a spark of understanding that reveals our resilience and our capacity to embrace all facets of our being.

The darkness, like a loving cocoon, offers us the space to breathe and rest. It is here that we can feel the quiet hum of our own essence, untainted by external demands. We are invited to lay down the weight we carry, to surrender fully to the unknown, and to trust in the wisdom that stirs within us. In these moments, we begin to understand that the stars we seek are not only above us—they are woven into the very fabric of our souls, waiting patiently to be seen and cherished.

Emerging from the Depths

The beauty of the darkness lies in its ability to deepen us. It becomes a mirror, reflecting both the stars that light our path and the vast, uncharted territories within us. It calls us to rest in the inky depths of our emotions, to let them flow over us like a gentle, velvety kiss, and to know that we are safe within this cocoon. Each moment of stillness, each pause, is a part of our journey—a soft lull before the dawn, a reminder that even in our most shadowed moments, we are held, loved, and whole.

When we emerge from the cocoon, we do so transformed, carrying with us the gifts of the shadows and the promise of light. The darkness does not diminish us; it nurtures us, allowing us to rise with greater depth, clarity, and grace.

When you think of darkness as a cocoon rather than something to fear, how does this perspective shift your feelings toward your current challenges or emotions?

How do you usually react when you face moments of darkness or uncertainty? Do you resist, or do you allow yourself to be held by it?

What gift might the darkness be offering you right now? How can you honor it as part of your journey?

SHADOWY MOUNTAINS

When the mountains become shadows
She claims her power

When the mountains become shadows
Her inner goddess arises

When the mountains become shadows
She runs with the wolves

When the Mountains become shadows
She becomes one with all

THE WILD WITHIN

Unleashing the Untamed Feminine

Darling, there is a wildness within you, an untamed pulse of life that has been with you since the beginning. Can you feel it stirring? It's the rhythm of the earth beneath your feet, the whisper of the wind in your hair, the roar of the ocean in your soul. This isn't something you need to search for; it's already yours. This wild, fierce, radiant energy is your birthright—it's you.

You were born with this primal force, this untamed spirit that longs to run free, to feel deeply, to live fully. It's the same wildness that moved your ancestors as they danced under the moonlight, the same fire that burned in their hearts as they walked the earth with courage and grace. And now, my love, it's your turn.

A Call to Remember

Let me remind you: you are not separate from nature—you are nature. The rivers mirror your flow, the mountains your strength, and the stars your light. When you allow yourself to connect with the world around you, you're not just stepping into nature; you're stepping into yourself.

Take a moment to breathe, my darling. Feel the air fill your lungs. Let it move through you, clearing the cobwebs of doubt and waking up the wild within. Can you feel it? The earth beneath you is alive, and so are you. You are part of this vast, beautiful web of existence, woven from the same threads as the stars, the seas, and the sky.

Reclaiming the Untamed Feminine

The wild woman within you is waiting. She's always been there, patiently calling you back to her. She's the voice in your soul that whispers, Trust me. Let go. You're safe. She's the one who dares you to run barefoot through the grass, to howl at the moon, to dance as though no one is watching.

To awaken her is to say yes to all of you—your strength and softness, your chaos and calm, your light and shadow. It's not about perfection; it's about presence. It's about trusting your instincts, listening to the wisdom of your body, and honoring the cycles that move through you.

Through sacred rituals—whether it's lighting a candle, moving your body, or simply breathing deeply—you can call her forth. Speak to her, my love. She's been waiting to hear your voice. Tell her you're ready to step into your power, to embrace the beauty of your becoming.

Stepping Into Your Wildness

Close your eyes for a moment and imagine this: You're running with wolves, their paws hitting the earth in rhythm with your heartbeat. The wind carries your hair as the stars shine above, and every part of you feels alive. You're free, untamed, radiant. This is who you are, darling. This is your truth.

So, let the wild within rise. Let her guide you, heal you, and remind you of your infinite power.

And if it's been too long, here's my gentle nudge: It's time. Time to howl at the moon. Time to dance under the stars. Time to let the wild within rise.

Let her run free, darling. Let you run free. You are a wild, beautiful force of nature, and the world is waiting to feel your magic.

> ***You are not just part of this earth;***
> ***you are the earth.***
> ***You're not just connected to the stars;***
> ***you are stardust.***

How can you reconnect with your untamed essence today?

What would it feel like to let your inner wild woman guide you, free of fear or judgment?

When was the last time you let yourself run free, unburdened by expectations?

WAVES OF EMOTIONS

It's like a wave
A wave full of thoughts
Feelings, memories, heaviness
Feels like I'm drowning
It's hard to breathe

I'm fighting, struggling
To keep my head above that water
The more I try
The deeper I drown

What if, when I hand myself over to the wave
To carry me
To wash over me

What if, when I trust
Allow myself to be held by that wave
She is teaching me to let go
To flow

I lay down
Handover myself
to be held
By my own waves

In an Ocean full of Emotions

THE OCEAN WITHIN

Life's waves often rise and fall within us—currents of emotion that carry the essence of our experiences. Thoughts, memories, and feelings crash like stormy seas, tugging us into their depths. These waves can feel overwhelming, as though we are adrift in an endless ocean, struggling to find our footing. But even in this turbulence, there exists an invitation—not to fight against the current but to surrender to its rhythm.

The Gift of Surrender

What if, instead of resisting, we trusted the ocean within us? What if, instead of tightening our grip, we softened into the ebb and flow of our emotions, allowing the tides to guide us? Surrender is not a sign of weakness; it is an act of courage. It is the knowing that life's rhythms are here to carry us, not drown us.

In surrender, there is profound strength. We let go not to lose ourselves but to align with the natural flow of life. The waves that once seemed insurmountable become gentle reminders that we are not separate from this vast ocean but part of its eternal dance.

Held by the Waters

When we surrender, we come to understand that the waters have been holding us all along. Every emotion—whether joy or sorrow, calm or chaos—belongs to us and shapes our journey. The waters of life cradle us in their embrace, carrying us toward healing, wisdom, and stillness.

Take a deep breath. Feel the rhythm of your emotions as they rise and fall like waves. Trust the ocean within you to guide your way.

Even in the stormiest seas, there is a shore waiting to welcome you.

An Invitation to Flow

Darling, you are not alone in this vast ocean. You are held by a force greater than your fears, carried by the waves you once thought would consume you. Let go of the need to control every tide; instead, trust the wisdom of the waters. Allow yourself to float, knowing that even in surrender, you are moving closer to the essence of who you truly are, and within that, you will always find your way home.

When the waves of emotion rise within you, how do you respond? Do you fight against them or allow yourself to be carried?

What would it feel like to trust your own waves to hold you? To let go and surrender to their wisdom?

How can you cultivate the courage to lay down your armor and flow with the tides of your emotions, knowing they are part of your sacred ocean within?

God can be found in anything

DIVINE CONNECTIONS

In the quiet moments, when the noise of the world fades and stillness wraps around us like a comforting cloak, there lies a sacred space within each of us. This space is not bound by time or place; it exists beyond the reach of distraction, where the divine whispers can be heard, soft and steady, like a heartbeat of the universe. It is here, in this sacred stillness, that the veil between the seen and unseen things, and we are reminded of the threads that bind us—not just to the cosmos, but to each other and to the infinite source of love and wisdom that flows through all things.

This is the space where the eternal and the ephemeral meet, where our earthly form dances with the divine. It is a sanctuary, a place of remembering, where we reconnect with the truth that we have never been separated. The divine has always been within and around us, waiting patiently for us to pause, to listen, and to feel its gentle presence.

A Call to Listening

This section invites you to journey deeper into this sacred space, to open your heart to the divine connection that resides within and weaves through the fabric of all creation. It is a call to surrender to the quiet nudges of your soul, those subtle yet powerful whispers that guide you toward your highest path.

In moments of prayer, meditation, or quiet reflection, these whispers become more audible. They may come as a soft voice, a warm sensation in your chest, or a sudden clarity that feels like a gift from the heavens. They are sacred dialogues, moments when the divine bends close to remind you that you are never alone.

This connection is not something you must seek or strive for; it is already yours. It is a birthright, an eternal thread that ties you to the great cosmic web. The divine speaks to you in countless ways—through the rustling of leaves, the glow of the moon, the words of a kind stranger, or the stillness of your own breath.

The Bridge to the Infinite

Imagine, for a moment, a bridge stretching from your heart to the infinite. This bridge glows with a soft, golden light, each step drawing you closer to the divine essence that has always been with you. As you cross, you feel the weight of the world fall away, replaced by a profound sense of peace and belonging.

Here, you are reminded that the divine is not distant or separate. It is in the breath you take, the ground beneath your feet, the pulse of your heart. It is in the quiet moments when you feel a sudden wave of love wash over you, unbidden and inexplicable. This is the divine reaching for you, reminding you that you are held, seen, and cherished.

An Eternal Embrace

This section is a sacred invitation—a gentle reminder of your inherent connection to the divine, your guides, and your own luminous soul. Let these words serve as a bridge to the spiritual realms, a pathway to the infinite love that seeks to illuminate your journey.

As you read, allow yourself to soften into this connection. Feel the love and wisdom that surround you like a warm embrace. Know that you are never alone. The divine walks with you, holding you in your moments of joy and sorrow, and guiding you even when the path feels uncertain.

You are a part of the cosmos, an irreplaceable thread in the great tapestry of existence. The light within you is a reflection of the light that illuminates the stars, and the love you carry is an echo of the infinite love that holds us all.

A Sacred Reminder

So, my love, take a breath and let yourself be held by these words. Let them remind you that you are always connected—to the divine, to the universe, to the boundless love that flows through all things. In this connection, you are whole, you are radiant, and you are forever guided.

As we journey through these chapters, you will discover my devotion to channeling messages from the cosmos, goddesses, and sacred spirits. For this chapter, I am deeply humbled to bring forth a message from Wiraqocha, the Great Creator. May these words carry the essence of infinite wisdom and divine love, awakening a deep remembrance of our sacred connection to a force far greater than we can imagine—a bond eternal with the universe itself.

A MESSAGE FROM WIRAQOCHA

Divine connection is not something to be sought, for it is already within you—it is the essence of who you are. From the moment your soul was born from the great spark of creation, you have carried the light of Wiraqocha within your heart, woven into your very being.

To feel the divine is to remember the stillness within you, the quiet whispers of your soul that call you back to love, to trust, to truth. It is the pulse of the earth beneath your feet, the rhythm of the stars above, the breath that flows through you, connecting you to all that is.

Do not look outward for the divine; instead, turn inward. In the depths of your heart, you will find the doorway to the infinite, the space where you and the cosmos meet as one. Divine connection is not a reaching, but a surrendering. It is the knowing that you are already whole, already held, already home.

Each prayer you speak, each offering you give, each act of love is a thread in the great web of reciprocity—Aini. As you give to the divine, the divine gives to you, for there is no separation, only the eternal flow of light, love, and life.

Remember, dear one, that you are never alone. The divine walks with you in every moment, in every breath. Feel this connection in the quiet of the morning, in the song of the wind, in the embrace of your own heart.

You are divine. You are sacred. You are the bridge between earth and sky, the vessel through which the light flows. Trust in this truth, and you will never lose your way.

In devotion and love, I walk with you.
Aini, always.

LURING WHISPERS

When I am deeply connected
to my soul's whispers
it feels like magic awakens
like the dust of a fae
that lures my mind
glamours me
and shows me the infinite beauty
within me
the sacredness
I need to see

AWAKENING THE MAGIC WITHIN

In the quiet moments, when the world's noise softens and fades away, a deeper voice begins to emerge—the voice of your soul. It is in these moments of stillness, when distractions rest and the busyness of life ebbs like a retreating tide, that the magic of your true essence begins to awaken. There is a beauty in this silence, a sacredness in the space where your soul's quiet whispers gently guide you back home.

Picture yourself stepping into a realm where the boundaries between the seen and unseen dissolve. Here, everything glows with a soft, ethereal light, as though the universe itself is speaking to you in its own language of wonder. The air feels alive with possibility, and every breath carries with it a sense of connection to something greater. In this space, you begin to feel the presence of something beyond the physical—a divine thread that has always been woven through your existence but may have been muted by the noise of everyday life. When you allow yourself to truly listen to these whispers, you are reminded of the infinite beauty that resides within you.

This beauty cannot be measured by the world's standards. It doesn't depend on appearances, accomplishments, or external validation. It is a light that shines from the depths of your being—a reflection of the love, wisdom, and divinity that exist in every corner of your soul.

A Journey of Remembering

Tuning into this deeper voice is not about finding something new; it is about remembering. It is about peeling back the layers of doubt, fear, and expectation to reveal the truth that has always been there: *You are enough.* In this sacred remembering, the limitations and doubts that once felt overwhelming begin to dissolve.

You reclaim the knowing that you are so much more than your physical form.

You are an expression of boundless potential, a radiant being of light capable of creating and transforming with every breath. In this space of connection, your soul invites you to see the world with fresh eyes. The mundane transforms into the magical. The smallest details—a drop of rain sliding down a windowpane, the gentle rustle of leaves in the wind—become sacred reminders of the wonder that exists all around you. And as you embrace this wonder, you begin to feel the sacredness of stillness, the profound beauty in simply being.

The Sacred Whispers Within

My love, your soul is always speaking to you, gently guiding you back to the truth of who you are. Its whispers are not loud or demanding; they are soft, tender, and patient, waiting for you to create the space to listen. These whispers remind you that you are always enough, always worthy, and always held by the infinite love that surrounds you.

To connect with this voice is to enter a sanctuary within yourself, a sacred space where you are safe, loved, and whole. In this sanctuary, the world's expectations fall away, leaving only the quiet truth of your being. It is here that you remember your essence, the light that has never dimmed, the beauty and wisdom that are timeless and eternal.

An Invitation to Awaken

So, my dear one, I invite you to pause for a moment. Close your eyes, take a deep breath, and allow yourself to sink into the stillness. Feel the whispers of your soul rising to meet you, each one a loving reminder of the infinite magic within you.

In times of doubt or uncertainty, you can always return to this space. You can always trust the quiet wisdom of your soul to guide you back to yourself. Let these whispers be your compass, your gentle anchor, as you navigate the ever-changing tides of life.

And as you journey forward, take this knowing with you:

the magic of your existence is not something you must seek or create—it is something you *are*. The infinite beauty and sacredness you long for have always lived within you.

Trust this connection, my love. Nurture it, cherish it, and allow it to remind you of the boundless potential that resides within us all. For it is in these moments of stillness when we truly listen to the whispers of our soul, that we awaken to the true magic of our existence.

How does it feel to witness the infinite beauty within yourself?

Reflect on the sacredness that is within you, waiting to be seen and embraced.

How can you cultivate a deeper connection to your soul's whispers in your daily life, allowing them to guide you toward a greater understanding of yourself and the world around you?

A SOUL'S PRAYER

I choose you to be here
Here on earth

I choose you to remember you
who you truly are

I choose you to be a love of light
love is your birthright
I choose you to create dreams
you are the creator
I choose you to embrace your deepest truth
I choose you to feel and embody all of those
feelings and emotions

Your body is my temple
your heart is my light
your mind is my vessel
your feelings are mine

I will always remember you why you are here
and who you truly are

I choose you to experience light and darkness
Like the moon

I remember you to celebrate and bless both
They are equally full of grace

I am not afraid of storms
and so you don't have to be

I will guide you
when you let me

I will let you feel
this deep connection to the universe
we are all made of stardust and galactic fragments

Listen deeply and you will hear my whisper

In love,

Your Soul

EMBRACING THE DIVINE CONNECTION

Within each of us lies a sacred sanctuary—a space untouched by the chaos of the outside world, where the essence of our being remains pure, timeless, and deeply connected to the divine. **This inner sanctuary is not separate from who we are; it *is* who we are.** It is the quiet, unshakable truth of our existence, inviting us to find peace, wisdom, and a deeper connection to our soul's purpose.

In the stillness of this sacred space, we sense the profound connection that binds us to the universe—a reminder that we are not separate from its vast and mysterious dance but an integral part of it. Here, in this sanctuary, the whispers of our soul grow louder. They carry messages of love, guidance, and insight, gently calling us back to the truth of who we are: divine beings, luminous and whole, capable of creating and experiencing the infinite magic of life.

The Journey of Connection

The journey of divine connection is not about escaping the world or retreating from its complexities; it is about embracing our place within it. We chose to be here, my love—to experience the duality of life, to feel the weight of its challenges and the lightness of its joys. This choice is a testament to our courage, a reminder that our souls longed to grow, evolve, and remember their divine essence through the human experience.

In embracing this connection, we recognize the sacredness of our earthly vessels. Our bodies become temples, our hearts radiant beacons of light, and our minds open channels through which divine wisdom flows. We carry within us the power of creation itself. With each thought, word, and action, we shape the reality we live, guided by the love and light that are our birthright.

Honoring the Duality of Life

To connect with the divine is to honor the duality of life—the light and the darkness, the joy and the sorrow, the moments of growth and the periods of stillness. It is to understand that both sides of the coin hold equal beauty and purpose. The light illuminates our path, while the darkness invites us inward to discover our strength and resilience.

Like the cycles of the moon, we move through phases, each with its very own lessons and grace. The fullness of the moon reminds us of our radiance, while its shadowed phases invite us to rest and reflect. Both are sacred, both are necessary, and both teach us to embrace the wholeness of our being.

The Presence of the Soul

Through this deep connection, we remember that we are never alone. Our souls are our most faithful companions, walking beside us in every moment. They remind us of our divine origins, whispering gently that we are always seen, always held, and always guided.

When we listen closely to these whispers, we find ourselves aligned with the greater flow of the universe. In this alignment, we feel the sacred rhythm of life moving through us—grounding us, connecting us, and filling us with peace. The soul's voice is always present, patiently waiting for us to pause, to breathe, and to receive its wisdom.

An Invitation to Remember

My love, I invite you to honor this sacred connection. Trust in the divine wisdom that resides within you and allow it to illuminate your path. When the world feels heavy, remember that your soul's light is unwavering, a beacon guiding you through the complexities of life.

Take a moment now to close your eyes, to place a hand over your heart, and to feel the quiet power of your soul. Let its whispers remind you of your purpose, your worth, and your infinite potential. You were chosen by the universe to be here, to create, to love, and to grow. Bask in this knowing, and let it fill you with the courage to embrace every aspect of your journey with grace and love.

Take a moment to bask in the love and wisdom of your soul, knowing that you are always supported and guided by its divine presence. You are never alone, my love. You are radiant, infinite, and deeply, divinely connected.

When you connect with the words of your soul, how does it feel to be chosen by the universe, to be reminded of your true essence and purpose?

How can you honor this connection and allow your soul's whisper to guide you on your journey?

…and so, she danced among the Stars of her own Universe…

CHILD OF THE UNIVERSE

I am a child of the universe
from stardust I am born

the unique sound of the earth
in every breath, every morn

from the stars and planets
to the depths of the sea

I am woven into this existence
as a part of eternity

let me embrace my cosmic roots
and dance among the stars
in the magic of the universe

BIRTHED BY THE STARS
COSMIC DNA

In the unimaginable infinity of the universe, each of us is a tiny speck of stardust, lovingly woven into the fabric of existence. From the moment of our birth, we are cradled by the cosmos, connected to the stars in ways that may defy understanding but resonate deeply within our souls. This connection, ancient and profound, flows through every aspect of our being, shaping the essence of who we are.

We are all celestial energetic beings

Each of us is a child of the universe, born from the same celestial materials that birthed galaxies, constellations, and the planets that light our skies. Within our very DNA, we carry the echoes of cosmic history—the remnants of ancient supernovae, the whispers of galaxies yet to be explored, and the energy that dances through the infinite expanse of space. This is the essence of our being, a sacred reminder that we are not separate from the universe but integral to its grand design.

The Song of the Cosmos

In our souls, the universe sings. It hums quietly beneath the surface of our awareness, a melody of interconnectedness that reminds us we are one—with each other, with the earth, and with the stars above. When we allow ourselves to pause and listen, we begin to remember. We remember that the same energy that ignites stars flows through our veins. The same creative force that shapes galaxies lives within us, guiding our path and illuminating our dreams.

This realization is a profound awakening—a recognition that we are not merely observers of the universe but participants in its unfolding story. Every breath we take, every thought we hold, every act of love and creation, adds to the symphony of existence. We are threads in the grand tapestry of life, weaving our unique colors and patterns into the infinite expanse of eternity.

The Adventure of Cosmic Connection

Exploring our cosmic roots is an adventure of self-discovery, a journey that invites us to see the world—and ourselves—with new eyes. It is a reminder that we are nourished by the same sacred energy that shapes galaxies and gives birth to new stars. This energy flows through us, grounding us in the beauty of existence while lifting us toward infinite possibility.

When we embody this connection, we open a channel to the universe's wisdom and guidance. We become attuned to its frequency, allowing its whispers to guide us with grace and ease. This connection is not abstract or distant—it is alive within us, accessible in every moment. It fuels our creativity, helps us manifest our wildest dreams, and offers us the courage to step into the fullness of who we are.

A Journey to the Heart of the Universe

Are you ready, my love, to open your heart and mind to a journey that leads you to the heart of the universe and back to the essence of your soul? This journey is not one of separation but of union, a remembering of your divine origin and the cosmic story that lives within you.

As you explore the mysteries of the universe, you will uncover hidden truths and unlock the secrets of your being. You will come to see that you are not merely an observer of the cosmos but a co-creator of its magic. You are part of its rhythm, its heartbeat, its endless dance of creation and transformation.

Honoring Your Cosmic Roots

Darling, you are made of stardust. Take a moment to feel the depth of this truth, to let it settle into your heart like a warm glow. You are woven from the very fabric of the cosmos, connected to the infinite and the eternal.

Place your hand over your heart and feel the beat of the universe pulsing through you. Honor your cosmic roots, for they ground you in the magnificence of existence and remind you that you are a radiant thread in the tapestry of life. You are here, not by chance, but by divine design, a beacon of light and love in the vastness of creation.

May you always remember your connection to the stars, and may this knowing will guide you on your journey through the beauty and wonder of life.

In which ways do you feel connected to the universe and its infinity? And how can you deepen this connection?

How does it feel to dance among the stars, embracing the divinity and cycles of the universe?

*Sing, my Love,
sing with me,
the eternal Song
of the Cosmos.*

DEVOTION

I pray to Myself
May I love & hold myself in every moment
May I be the love of my life

I pray to Pachamama
May she ground me, heal me, hold me

I pray to Mama Moon
May she teach me that I don't need to shine bright
at any time and show me how to celebrate my
shadow side

I pray to Father Sun
May the sun brighten up my paths, nourish me
with warmth and remind me of my own light

I pray to the Elements
May the wind bring me clarity and carry away what
no longer serves me

May the water wash away my pain and let me heal through the sacredness

May the fire lighten up my darkness and help me burn away what I no longer need

May the earth help me to stay grounded and connected, deep-rooted and secure

May spirit remind me that I am a part of the universe and always divinely guided

I pray to the Divine

May divine energy flow through me in every moment and remind me that I am filled with divinity and grace

So mote it be!

Thank you! Thank you! Thank you!

DEVOTION
A PATH TO GRACE

My love, in the noise and chaos of the world, it's so easy to lose sight of the sacredness that resides within and around you. But when you pause—when you allow stillness to wrap around you like a comforting embrace—you begin to hear the gentle whispers of the divine. These moments of connection are an invitation to remember, to return to the sacred beauty of devotion—a practice that nourishes your soul and draws you closer to the infinite love that holds you.

Prayer is one of the most tender expressions of devotion. It is not bound by form, tradition, or time but flows freely from the heart, weaving together your gratitude, intentions, and connection to the vast, infinite universe. Through prayer, you honor yourself, the Earth, the elements, the celestial dance of the stars, and the divine forces that flow through all things. It is a sacred sanctuary, a soft embrace where you can ground yourself in love, release what no longer serves you, and open your heart fully to the wisdom, grace, and guidance of the universe.

The Essence of Devotion

Devotion begins with the simplest yet most profound act: **loving yourself.** When you pray for yourself, you are honoring the divine light that lives within you. You are reminding yourself that you are worthy of love, grace, and compassion, not because of what you do but simply because you exist. You are a vessel of light, capable of holding yourself with tenderness through every twist and turn of life.

This love extends outward, connecting you to Pachamama—our beloved Mother Earth. She cradles you with her steady presence, grounding you in her rhythms and offering her endless support. When you ground yourself in her embrace, you feel her love flowing through you, reminding you that you are never alone.

Honoring the Celestial and the Elements

Darling, look to the celestial forces that guide you. Mama Moon, with her luminous cycles, teaches you that it's okay to retreat into the shadows, to rest, and to let yourself be held in the quiet beauty of your darker phases. She reminds you that you don't need to shine brightly at all times. Her presence is a gentle invitation to embrace the fullness of your being—the light and the shadow alike.

Father Sun offers his radiant warmth, illuminating your path and nourishing your spirit. He whispers to you of your own brilliance, of the light that you carry and the courage it takes to let it shine. Together, they teach you the balance of life, the harmony of rest and radiance, of surrender and creation.

The elements, too, are sacred guides. The wind brushes against your cheek, carrying away the weight you no longer need to bear. Water washes over you, cleansing and renewing your spirit.

Fire flickers within you, burning away what no longer serves you and igniting transformation. Earth grounds you, holding you steady when the world feels uncertain. Each element whispers its wisdom to you, inviting you to trust in the flow of life.

An Invitation to Devotion

My love, devotion is not a task or obligation—it is a sacred act of remembering.

When you pray, you are not asking for something outside of yourself; you are reconnecting with the infinite that has always lived within you.

You are aligning with the gentle current of divine energy that flows through all things, a current that carries you with grace and love.

Take a moment to place your hand over your heart. Unclench your jaw, relax your shoulders, and take a deep breath. Close your eyes and feel the steady rhythm of your breath, the quiet strength of your being. In this stillness, you are held—by the universe, by the Earth, by the love that surrounds you.

Darling, may you carry this sense of devotion with you as a sacred thread that ties you to the beauty of existence. Through prayer, may you find a refuge, a sanctuary, and a reminder that you are always held, always guided, and always loved.

And always remember, devotion and prayer don't need a specific ritual or grand gestures. Start by simply saying "***I love you***" to yourself, mean it, and feel it.

How can you create tender moments of devotion in your daily life, where you pause to honor the sacred?

In what ways do you feel the divine speaking to you—through the elements, the stars, or the quiet whispers of your soul?

When you pray, what does it feel like to connect to the infinite love that flows within and around you?

GODDESS OF THE UNIVERSE

I shower myself

With the unconditional love & grace

From the mother of the universe,

Goddess of the Stars,

Home of my Soul

Fill my heart and soul with your divine essence of love and grace

Emerge my heart with the source of the galaxy

Melting my soul into her arms

And so it is

THE COSMIC DANCE OF LOVE AND GRACE

A sacred space exists, where the boundaries between the self and the universe dissolve, and we are invited to bathe in the luminous glow of cosmic love and grace. It is in these moments of surrender and openness—when we feel our place in the infinite web of existence—that we remember we are not separate from the cosmos but intricately woven into its radiant fabric.

At the heart of this connection lies Mayu, the celestial goddess of the Milky Way. In Andean mythology, Mayu is the sacred river of stars, flowing through the heavens as an eternal thread that binds the universe together. Her presence embodies nurturing, feminine energy—the cradle of creation and the source of infinite love. To honor Mayu is to honor the galaxy itself, a reflection of the divine grace that moves through every corner of existence.

Mayu's essence reminds us that we are stardust come alive, that the divine flows within us as surely as it flows through the galaxies. Her cosmic river holds the memories of ancient worlds, the birth of stars, and the endless cycles of creation and transformation. She invites us to step into this river, to let its current carry us closer to the heart of the universe and, in doing so, closer to ourselves.

A Sacred Dance

Within the depths of our being, we carry the imprint of the stars—the ancient echoes of galaxies born and extinguished, the rhythms of cosmic tides that ebb and flow across eternity. With each breath, we inhale the essence of the universe, filling ourselves with its limitless potential. As we exhale, we release what no longer serves us, surrendering to the gentle rhythm of the cosmic dance.

To dance with the universe is to remember our place as both participants and creators. We are not mere observers of its infinite beauty; we are active threads in its unfolding tapestry. Within our souls burns the spark of the divine—a radiant flame that illuminates not only our path but the dark, unseen corners of the cosmos. This realization is the deepest truth: we are not separate from the divine; we are its living, breathing expression.

A Moment of Surrender

Take a moment, my love, to close your eyes. Tune into the soft rhythm of the cosmos pulsing through your veins, a rhythm older than time itself. Feel the tender embrace of Mayu, the mother of the universe, as she cradles you in her infinite arms. Her whispers are ancient truths, filling the depths of your soul with love, grace, and the knowing that you are held, always.

In this moment, let yourself dissolve into the cosmic river. Feel your heart melt into its currents, your soul merging with the stars.

May you always remember, my love, that you are a child of the stars, a thread in the infinite tapestry of life. You are held, cherished, and cradled in the arms of the cosmos, forever connected to the radiant river of Mayu and the boundless love she offers. Take a moment to honor the sacredness of your being.

> ***In this space, you are infinite.***
> ***You are boundless.***
> ***You are one with the cosmos.***

How can you deepen your practice of self-love and self-acceptance, honoring every facet of who you are?

What would it feel like to trust the cosmic rhythm that flows through your life, surrendering fully to its grace?

When you connect with the divine energy of the universe, what truths arise within you?

EMBRACING THE SELF

A Sacred Homecoming to Your True Essence

In the tender stillness of these pages, you are invited into a sanctuary of self—an intimate space where you can lay down the burdens of judgment and expectation. This chapter is an invitation to reconnect with the deepest, most authentic parts of yourself. It is a gentle reminder that the journey inward is not a quest for perfection but a sacred act of radical love and acceptance.

An Invitation to See Yourself Clearly

So often, we move through life wearing masks, adjusting to what we believe is expected of us. But here, in this sacred space, you are encouraged to let the masks fall away. You are invited to look into the mirror of your soul and see yourself as you truly are: a being of infinite worth and boundless beauty. This is not about fixing or improving—it is about embracing. The light and the shadow, the joy and the sorrow, the triumphs and the trials—all of it is you, and all of it is worthy of love.

The Gentle Art of Coming Home

Coming home to yourself is not a grand destination but a series of small, tender moments—a softening into the present, a quiet acknowledgment of your feelings, a whispered reminder that you are enough. It is a journey that asks for your patience and your grace, inviting you to embrace the ebb and flow of emotions, memories, and truths as they arise. Each step on this path is a reclamation, a weaving together of all the pieces you once believed were broken or unworthy.

Honoring Your Wholeness

To embrace yourself fully is to recognize that you are already whole, even in moments of doubt or fear. Nothing is missing, nothing broken. You are a living mosaic, each fragment of your being contributing to the masterpiece of your existence. This chapter is a celebration of that wholeness—

a reminder that your worth is not conditional, your beauty not diminished by flaws, and your light not extinguished by shadows.

A Mirror for Your Soul

As you turn these pages, let them reflect back to you the truth of who you are. Let them remind you of the courage it takes to be vulnerable, the strength it requires to embrace your imperfections, and the beauty that shines when you step fully into your authenticity. This is not just a journey of self-reflection; it is a journey of self-remembering. You are not becoming someone new; you are coming home to the person you've always been.

Welcome home, dear soul. May you walk this path with tenderness, curiosity, and a deep sense of wonder for the being you are rediscovering. And may you remember, always, that you are enough—just as you are, in this very moment.

As you already know about me, I'm working deeply with the energies of the cosmos and Goddesses.

For this chapter, I am the vessel for a message from Aphrodite, the Goddess of unconditional divine love.

Open your heart my love and let yourself be cradled by the divine love of Aphrodite.

You are Love

and

You are loved

MESSAGE FROM APHRODITE

My dearest child of the stars and the earth,

Feel my presence as a gentle tide washing over your soul, whispering truths your heart already knows. You are a masterpiece—a living, breathing expression of divine love. Every curve, every shadow, every scar tells the story of your becoming, and oh, how beautiful you are in your wholeness.

Do not seek perfection; it is a fleeting mirage. Instead, find grace in your imperfections, for they are what make you real, what make you alive. Your essence is not defined by how others see you, but by the way you choose to see yourself. Stand before the mirror and let your gaze soften. Look not with judgment, but with love. See the light that dances in your eyes and the wisdom that flows through your being. **You are more than enough, my love.**

Let the tender rhythm of your breath remind you that you are connected to the pulse of the universe. With every inhale, call in the love that surrounds you; with every exhale, release the lies that tell you otherwise. You are worthy of love—not because of what you do, but simply because you are.

Celebrate yourself, not just in moments of triumph, but in the quiet, ordinary seconds where your heart beats steadily, carrying you forward. Adorn yourself with kindness, drape your soul in self-compassion, and let your inner beauty radiate outward. Know that you are held, cherished, and adored by forces far greater than you can imagine. And when the world feels heavy, return to this truth:

You are love, you are light, and you are sacred. I see you, and I celebrate all that you are.

Rise, my darling, as the goddess within you wakes, for she is ready to dance, to love, and to embrace all that life offers.

With infinite grace and devotion,

- *Aphrodite*

You are divine.

DANCE WITH EMOTIONS

Let yourself be merged
With all emotions
Surrender into them

Welcome them all
With an open heart & widened wings

Lay them down
on the great mother's altar

Let yourself be reminded that
the state of natural happiness is
to allow yourself
to feel Everything
between Above & Below
and beyond all of that

You are a cyclic being
A soul in a human body
You are here
to feel all these human emotions

There's no good or bad emotion
It's just an emotion
There's no right or wrong way to feel it

Feeling it
is the only path you need to walk
Let them be free

Uncage them
Let your feelings and emotions get wild

Untamed
Like a growling thunderstorm
Let them be calm and kind, a gently flowing river
or bright and bold and shiny
Let them be whatever they want to be

Emotions to be felt

EMOTIONAL DANCE

In this sacred lifetime, where your soul chooses to embody the human experience, emotions become the vibrant threads weaving the fabric of your being. They are the colors painting the canvas of your inner world, offering you the most intimate connection to your truth. Yet, in a world that often whispers for us to mute or control our feelings, it's easy to forget the profound wisdom and beauty emotions carry.

An Invitation to Feel Fully

Dearest one, emotions are not here to overwhelm you; they are here to guide you. Each tear, every burst of laughter, the ache of sorrow, and the spark of joy—all are sacred messengers. They whisper the truths your heart already knows and invite you to lean into the fullness of being alive.

They are not meant to be silenced but held with tenderness, allowing them to teach you and transform you.

These words were born in a moment of release, after a much-needed good cry—or perhaps a cry-laugh, one of those rare, messy moments where you're unsure if you're weeping or laughing or both at once. A moment where pain, relief, and joy collide, creating the most beautiful chaos, and painting your soul with hues only such rawness can bring. This is how I felt when these words found me—a soul-deep reminder that emotions, in all their forms, are here to be acknowledged and cherished.

To cry, to laugh, to rage, and to exhale deeply is not just healing—it is honoring the sacred dance of your soul in this human form. **This is the raw beauty of being alive.**

Emotions as Sacred Messengers

Your emotions are not random; they are sacred allies, guiding you back home to yourself. They are the storms and rivers of your inner landscape, clearing away the debris of doubt, fear, and old wounds. Like waves kissing the shore, they cleanse and renew, creating space for growth and light to emerge.

Often, we are taught to suppress certain emotions, labeling them as "negative" or unworthy of our attention. But what if every feeling was simply energy in motion, yearning to be felt and freed? The joy that dances in your chest and the sorrow that tightens your throat—both belong. Both are worthy of your compassion. By honoring each emotion, you allow yourself to move closer to the truth of your being.

Surrendering to the Dance

To surrender to your emotions is an act of courage, my love. It is laying your heart bare on the altar of the Great Mother, trusting her to hold you through the chaos and calm alike. It is remembering that happiness is not the absence of sorrow, but the willingness to feel it all. To feel deeply is to live deeply, and in this surrender, you meet the fullness of who you are.

Imagine your emotions as dance partners, guiding you through moments of stillness and motion. Some days, they may twirl you in a waltz of joy. On other days, they may sway you in the tender embrace of grief. Each step, each movement, is an invitation to know yourself more deeply, to trust the rhythm of your soul's journey.

The Beauty of Being Human

My love, you are not broken by your emotions. You are made whole by them. You are a cyclic being—a soul housed in a body designed to feel. There is no "right" or "wrong" way to experience your feelings. They are not meant to be tamed or judged but embraced with an open heart. Allow your emotions to be as wild as a thunderstorm or as gentle as a flowing river. Let them take the shape they need, for in their freedom lies your liberation.

In this dance, you are not alone. The Great Mother cradles you, her whispers reminding you that every tear, every smile, every shiver of vulnerability is sacred. You are held, always, in her infinite love.

Coming Home to Yourself

As you surrender to this emotional dance, you come home to yourself over and over again. You remember that you are both the storm and the calm, the ebb and the flow. You are the starry night sky, vast enough to hold every emotion, every flicker of light and shadow.

Let yourself feel, dear soul. Let yourself be moved by the waves of your humanity. In this dance, you are not lost.

How does it feel to embrace your emotions as sacred messengers?

Can you think of a time when releasing your emotions brought you clarity or healing?

What would it look like to allow yourself to feel fully, without judgment or resistance?

The tears will come when they're ready.

They may not need to be forced but simply invited.

SHE

She sats with herself
Cried healing tears
Loved herself with pleasure

She laughs
She falls
She rises

She is me
and
I am she

RADICAL SELF-ACCEPTANCE

A Homecoming to Your Heart

In the whirlwind of daily tasks, endless to-do lists, and responsibilities, we often lose ourselves to the demands and expectations of the world around us. We strive for perfection, crave validation, and seek acceptance from others, all while neglecting the most important relationship of all—the one we have with ourselves.

But what if true happiness and fulfillment were not found in external achievements, but in the simple act of loving and accepting ourselves, just as we are? What if, within the depths of your being, there was already an endless wellspring of love, resilience, and potential waiting for you to tap into?

The Sacred Power of Self-Love

Radical self-acceptance is not about fixing or changing yourself; it's about honoring every part of who you are—your light and your shadow, your joy and your pain. It is a declaration of love for the wholeness of your being, a reminder that you are not broken, but beautifully human.

These words of "SHE" came to me during a time of a deep and soul-stirring transformation in my own life, whispering that self-love is the foundation upon which all healing and growth are built. True liberation begins from within. It starts when we sit with ourselves, facing our fears and insecurities with tenderness, and embracing every part of who we are—flaws, scars, and all. Only then can we experience the fullness of healing and wholeness.

Honoring the Human Spirit

At its core, this journey is a celebration of the human spirit—a reminder of the vast resilience that lies within each of us. It acknowledges the beauty of our shared experiences, from moments of laughter to times of sorrow, and honors the ever-unfolding path of self-discovery.

But how do we embark on this journey? How do we learn to love and accept ourselves completely, without conditions or comparisons? Especially in a world where we're allured and influenced by how we 'should' look, act, or even how we 'should' live. But here, in this sacred space, there are no 'shoulds.' There is only a gentle reminder to come home to yourself, just as you are.

Creating Space for Wholeness

The answer lies in cultivating presence and mindfulness. Radical self-acceptance is about creating space for yourself—space to breathe, to reflect, and to simply be. It's about letting go of the idea that your worth depends on your achievements or the validation of others. Your worth is intrinsic. It exists simply because you do.

Through practices like meditation, journaling, and gentle self-expression, we begin to peel back the layers of doubt and fear. We rediscover the light within us and learn to hold space for our emotions. In this sacred process, we remember that the most profound love we will ever experience is the love we give ourselves.

Embracing the Journey

So let us embrace this path, my darlings. Let us sit with our emotions and let the healing tears flow. Let us laugh with abandon, stumble without shame, and rise again and again—each moment an invitation to grow, to transform, and to love ourselves more deeply.

Know this: **you are not alone.** Your journey is unique, yet it is also shared. She is me, and She is You. Together, we walk this path toward wholeness. **We are one.**

You are whole, my love. You are worthy.
And you are already enough.
Let your self-love be your greatest revolution.
I see you.

Take a moment to reflect on your own sacred journey.

Can you remember a time when your tears became a healing balm, washing away the pain and uncovering strength you didn't know you had?

How do you tenderly hold space for yourself during moments of vulnerability, allowing your soul's voice to emerge?

What would it feel like to fully embrace your divine essence, flaws and all, as the masterpiece you already are?

LURKING FIRE

The fire in you is lurking
It lurks to burn

Don't be afraid of it
Grab it
Feel it
Let it expand
Let it grow

Above you & beyond
Let yourself swathed by it

It is your own power
Your inner flame
Your energy
Your magic

Reclaim it

IGNITE THE FIRE WITHIN

There is a fire that lives inside you, burning with the essence of your being—a fierce yet tender force that holds the truth of who you are. This flame is your life force, your vitality, your passion, and your magic. **It is the spark of divinity that calls you home to yourself, inviting you to embrace all that you are**. It dances, waiting patiently for you to turn inward, to see it, to feel it, and to honor its sacred power.

This inner fire is not something to tame; it is something to cherish. Like the wild flames that flicker in nature, your fire is a balance of creation and transformation, destruction and renewal. It burns away the illusions and doubts that weigh heavy on your spirit, clearing the path for your truth to shine through. It illuminates the spaces within you that long to be seen, bringing warmth to the tender parts of your heart that yearn for love. When you choose to meet this fire within, you are choosing to step into your power.

And yes, my love, it takes courage. To embrace your inner flame is to sit with its intensity, to listen to its whispers, and to face the shadows it reveals. But this fire is not your enemy; it is your guide, your strength, your ally. It holds the wisdom of transformation, showing you how to release the old stories and step boldly into the fullness of your being.

Nurture Your Fire

Tending to your inner fire means creating space for your passions, your dreams, and your truth. It's about letting your fire breathe, allowing it to expand and illuminate every part of your life. It fuels your creativity, ignites your desires, and leads you toward your deepest purpose. This flame, when nurtured, becomes a light that not only warms your soul but inspires others to embrace their own. But remember, darling, this is not a fire to control. It is a force to flow with, a sacred energy to honor. Let it teach you how to release what no longer serves you—old wounds, fears, and the weight of expectations. Let it guide you to create a life that feels authentic, aligned, and deeply fulfilling. This fire within you is not just a source of passion; it is the compass that points you back to your truth.

As you tend to your inner flame, notice how it illuminates your path. Feel its warmth reminding you of your resilience and your infinite potential. You are a creator, a force of nature, and this fire is your power. It asks you to live boldly, to love fiercely, and to trust the brilliance of your light.

A Sacred Reminder

Your fire is not just a spark—it is a radiant force. It is the light that guides you, the strength that sustains you, and the love that fuels your soul. Embrace it fully, darlings. Let it burn brightly, and trust that it will always light your way.

Take a moment to close your eyes and visualize your inner fire. Watch as it flickers and glows, its warmth reaching every corner of your being.

What does it feel like to stand in its light, to let it shine without hesitation?

What fuels your inner fire the most? Is it creativity, connection, solitude, or something else entirely? Reflect on the moments that make your soul burn brightest.

What old stories, fears, or doubts might your fire be asking you to release? How can you lovingly let them go to make space for new possibilities?

Trust me, my Dear,
You are never lost.

MADNESS

I've been gone through madness

Only to find myself
Over and over again

When I find myself
I find my soul

I'm coming home

FINDING HOME THROUGH MADNESS

Sweet soul, have you ever felt lost in the chaos of your own mind? As if the world around you is spinning too fast, and the ground beneath you feels unsteady? Those moments, the ones that leave you gasping for clarity in a sea of uncertainty, are not signs of weakness or failure. They are sacred invitations—gentle nudges from the universe to pause, to surrender, and to meet yourself in a way you never have before.

The Sacred Passage of Madness

What if I told you that the moments you feel most untethered are the very moments guiding you home? The chaos you feel inside is not something to fear or silence—it's a conversation, a sacred dialogue between your soul and the parts of you yearning to be seen. Madness is not the villain; it is the teacher, here to unravel the masks you've worn and reveal the truth you've been carrying all along.

In this tender unraveling, you are not breaking; you are shedding. Shedding the stories you no longer need, the identities you've outgrown, and the weight that was never yours to carry. And when all that falls away, you are left with the essence of who you are—a radiant being of light, love, and infinite possibility.

You Are Not Lost

The chaos may feel like it's pulling you under, but I promise you, love, you are not lost. You are being held, even in the wildest storms. This madness you feel is not a punishment; it is a portal, one that leads you back to the heart of your being. And while the journey may be messy, confusing, and even painful at times, it is also divinely beautiful.

Take a deep breath with me. Place your hand on your heart. Feel the rhythm of life pulsing within you. That is your home. That is your soul, whispering its truth, calling you back to yourself.

Trust its wisdom. Trust its love.

Coming Home to Yourself

Coming home is not a single moment or a destination. It is a soft, sacred practice of remembering—again and again—that you are whole. It is the gentle exhale that comes when you realize you do not need to have all the answers or carry the weight of the world alone.

Sweet one, let yourself rest. Let yourself be held by the rhythm of life. The times when you feel most lost are often the times when you are closest to being found. **The chaos is not here to break you; it is here to reveal you**—to remind you of the strength, beauty, and divinity that has always been yours.

The Gift of Madness

Madness is not the end. It is the beginning of something new, something sacred. It is the soul's way of bringing you back to your truest essence. So, when the world feels heavy and your mind feels tangled, know this: you are never truly lost. You are simply being called to pause, to breathe, and to listen to the quiet voice within that whispers, "I am here. I have always been here."

Let these words hold you. Let them remind you that the stars are not only above you but within you. And when the storm calms and the skies clear, you will see the beauty that was always there, waiting to guide you home.

I am never lost; I am always on my way home.

What moments in your life have felt like a storm, and how did you find your way through?

When you think of "home," what feelings, sensations, or memories rise to the surface?

How can you embrace the chaos as a teacher, trusting it to guide you closer to your truth?

Rise, Darling, Rise

RAYS OF LIGHT

A Phase of Illumination

Under the luminous glow of the Full Moon, we are called to witness the culmination of our inner journey. The Full Moon, with her radiant brilliance, stands as a symbol of reflection, wholeness, and illumination. She invites us to celebrate the light we carry and the growth that has emerged from the shadows we've embraced.

Embracing the Dance Between Shadow and Light

Emerging from the tender cocoon of darkness, we find ourselves transformed. The light now streaming through is not here to erase the shadows but to dance with them, revealing hidden beauty and casting new shapes. It reminds us that every shadow holds a seed of dawn, and every spark of light is born from the darkness.

The Warmth of Wholeness

In this sacred phase, we honor the parts of ourselves that longed for the light and the courage it took to walk through the shadows. This journey is not about arriving at a perfect destination but about embracing the truth of who we are—whole, radiant, and beautifully human.

An Invitation to Step Into Your Light

These pages are an invitation to let the rays of light gently touch the corners of your soul. They are a reflection of hope, resilience, and self-compassion—a call to bask in the warmth of your own brilliance. Let the light guide you, not as a fleeting moment, but as a steady companion on your journey, illuminating the beauty of your path.

And remember, my darling, the light is not something to hope for—it is something to know. Just as the sun rises without fail each morning, so too will you rise. You may waver, stumble, or feel the weight of shadows, but the spark within you remains eternal. Listen not to the voice of doubt but to the knowing deep within your soul, the one that whispers:

**You will rise, just as the sun does—
again, and again, and again.**

My journey is deeply rooted in the sacred energies of the cosmos and the divine archetypes that guide us. My soul feels a sacred connection to Andean mythology, where the stories of the Apus, Pachamama, and Wiraqocha have awakened something ancient within me.

For this chapter, I am humbled to serve as the vessel for a message from Ch'aska, the radiant Goddess of Light. She is the essence of Tayta Inti's (Father Sun) eternal warmth and the soft, nurturing glow that illuminates our path forward.

Ch'aska carries the wisdom of cycles—the sun rising and setting, the balance of light and shadow within us all. Her light tenderly reveals what we may have hidden from ourselves, urging us to embrace the beauty of our wholeness.

My Love, open yourself to her golden embrace. Feel her light pouring into your heart as a reminder that even in your darkest night, the promise of dawn always remains.

A MESSAGE FROM CH'ASKA

Goddess of the Sun

Beloved, my rays find you in every shadow, in every corner where you may have forgotten your light. I do not shine to chase away the darkness but to remind you that it, too, is part of the whole.

You are the dawn and the dusk, the sunlight and the moonbeam. Within you lives the harmony of cycles, the balance of light and shadow. When you fear that the shadows will overcome you, remember: they are merely the places where my rays have yet to touch.

Step boldly into your light, not to banish what is dark, but to integrate it. For even in the darkest nights, my promise of light remains eternal, just as you are eternal. You carry my essence, golden and infinite, within your heart.

Know this: **the brilliance you seek is not beyond you—it is you.** Let your words, your actions, and your creations be an extension of this truth. And as you shine, you will awaken the light in others, one ray at a time.

With love eternal,

Ch'aska

Shine bright, Darling

You are the Sun

BENEATH ALL MY LAYERS

Beneath all my layers of pain, grief, and anger
There's pure light

Deep inside my heart
I keep the source
Of pure love

It is infinitely

I open my heart
I open my source
To love, light, healing

For me

For you

For the world

For every living being

UNVEILING THE LIGHT WITHIN

The Eternal Flame of Your Soul

Deep within the sacred sanctuary of your being lies a treasure far greater than you can imagine—a radiant light that burns with the brilliance of a thousand stars. This light, untouched by the weight of the world, is your eternal essence, your source of hope, love, and healing. Even in the moments when darkness feels all-consuming, this light remains unwavering, patiently waiting to illuminate your path.

Layers That Obscure, but Never Diminish

Life, with all its trials and challenges, can sometimes dim our awareness of this inner brilliance. Layers of pain, grief, and anger often build like clouds around the sun, obscuring the warmth and glow of our true essence. Yet, even beneath these burdens, your light never fades. It is a constant, a beacon that whispers of your inherent grace, your capacity for love, and your infinite resilience.

The Sacred Journey of Unveiling

To unveil this light is to embark on the most sacred of journeys—a journey of self-transformation. It calls for courage and tenderness as you begin to peel away the layers that no longer serve you. It invites you to gently hold the parts of yourself that carry pain, offering them love and compassion, and to release what weighs you down. This unveiling is not an act of erasure but of alchemy, where you transform your heaviest shadows into shimmering light.

The Courage to Embrace Your Radiance

This journey is not a race, nor does it have a destination. It is a sacred unfolding, a return to your divine essence. Each step you take brings you closer to the truth of who you are—a being of infinite love, born from the stars, here to create, to heal, and to thrive.

The path may not always be easy. There will be moments of discomfort, times when you feel like retreating into the safety of old patterns. But know this: you are never walking alone. With each step, you are held by the infinite wisdom of the universe and guided by the radiant flame that burns within you. Trust in its warmth, let it soothe your weary soul and allow it to remind you of your strength.

Honoring the Light Within

So, my dear one, take a moment to close your eyes and breathe deeply. Feel the glow of your inner light, gently flickering beneath the surface, waiting for your embrace. Trust that no matter how far you've wandered from yourself, you can always come home to this sacred place within your heart.

You are the light, my dear, never forget that.

What emotions arise when you imagine uncovering your inner light and allowing it to shine freely?

How might you nurture this light within you—through quiet moments of reflection, acts of self-love, or simply trusting in its presence?

What steps can you take today to peel back even one layer and move closer to the luminous essence of who you are?

RECLAIMING HUMANESS

With every breath I take
I am reclaiming my humanness
I connect to that human being I am
I remember myself how it feels to be a human

With every word I speak
I reclaim my inner voice
I connect to my truth

With every star is see
I am reclaiming the magic to open portals of my soul
I connect with the universe

With every prayer
I reclaim my blessings
I fill my body with grace

And so it is

BEING HUMAN

In a world that often glorifies perfection, it can be easy to forget the sacred beauty of simply being human. We are constantly encouraged to strive for flawlessness, yet it is within our imperfections that we find the deepest truths of our existence. Beneath the surface of our flaws lies something profound—a divinity that transcends our outer struggles and connects us to the magic of life itself.

To be human is to embody both the light and the shadow. It is to navigate the highs and lows, to experience the full spectrum of emotions, and to find meaning in the ordinary moments that shape our days. Reclaiming our humanity means embracing this complex, messy, and beautiful journey with every breath, word, and thought.

With every breath, we reconnect to the essence of being alive. It is a reminder of the simple yet profound gift of existence—a moment-to-moment renewal that anchors us in the present. Our breath is a gateway to our innermost self, a reminder that being here, now, is itself a miracle.

Similarly, each word we speak carries the power to reclaim our truth. In a world full of noise, finding our authentic voice is an act of self-liberation. Through our words, we shape reality, sharing our stories, beliefs, and desires. Speaking from the heart allows us to shine as our true selves, unapologetically embracing who we are.

The power of observation reveals the magic all around us. By simply beholding the stars, the leaves, or the shifting clouds, we reconnect with the vastness of the universe. In that moment of awe, we remember that we are not separate from the world but part of a cosmic dance that stretches across time and space. Every glimpse of beauty is a portal to our soul, reminding us of our place within the grand tapestry of existence.

Prayer, too, holds a unique power in this journey of reclamation. Through prayer—whether spoken or felt silently within—we express our gratitude, our hopes, and our intentions. It is a way to acknowledge the divine presence that flows through all things, including ourselves. By filling our bodies and minds with grace, we reclaim the blessings that surround us, often unnoticed.

Embracing the Gift of Imperfection

Our imperfections are not flaws to be erased; they are sacred markings of a life lived fully. To stumble, to cry, to laugh, and to love—this is the dance of being human. These moments of vulnerability and triumph create the mosaic of our soul's expression, making us beautifully, uniquely ourselves.

In the embrace of imperfection, we discover resilience. When we allow ourselves to feel deeply, to let the cracks show, we create space for light to enter. Each scar becomes a story, a lesson, a testament to our strength. By reclaiming these pieces of ourselves, we step closer to wholeness—not a flawless ideal, but a wholeness that honors every part of our journey.

The Dance of Connection

Being human is also about connection—our sacred bond with the divine, the earth, and one another. When we touch the soil with bare hands, walk beneath the stars, or share our hearts with other beings, we weave threads of connection that ground us in the shared experience of life. These moments remind us that we are never truly alone.

Our humanness invites us to both give and receive love. It is in the exchange of compassion, kindness, and vulnerability that we find the truest reflection of ourselves. By reaching out, holding space for others, and allowing ourselves to be held, we reclaim the sacred gift of connection.

An Invitation to Reclaim

As you continue on your journey, I invite you to reflect on the power of each breath, each word, each moment of observation, and each prayer. Notice the magic that exists in the small, often overlooked corners of your day.

Feel the heartbeat of the earth beneath your feet and the rhythm of life moving through you.

In reclaiming your humanness, you will rediscover the sacred truth that has always been within you: that you are whole, you are divine, and you are enough—just as you are.

How does it feel to remember about the magic and grace within you?

How can you honor and nurture these connections in your daily life, allowing them to guide you on your own path?

YOU ARE ENOUGH

You do not have to prove yourself to anyone.
You know who you are.
You carry the whole universe inside of you
like a shimmering Opal,
colorful like a field of flowers
deep like the ocean
filled with unconditional Love

You are the source of love

Listen to me darling, I know all the answers
and so you do
I hear all your prayers

Trust me
I love you
I forgive you
Thank you

You are enough & exactly where you mean to be

Love, Your Soul

You are the Source of Love

YOUR DIVINE ESSENCE

Deep within you, beyond the noise of the outside world, lies a sacred place where your truest self resides. It is here, at the core of your being, that you will find the eternal flame of your soul—a flame that burns with the wisdom, love, and light of the divine. This essence, pure and untouchable, is a reflection of who you truly are, beyond the fleeting challenges and distractions of life.

When you pause to listen, your soul speaks to you in whispers so tender: You are enough. These words ripple through the depths of your being, a sacred reminder of your inherent worth and completeness. You carry this truth within you at all times, even when the world around you makes you feel otherwise.

My dear one, you are like a shimmering opal—multi-faceted and alive with vibrant colors, each facet revealing a part of your divine nature. You are a unique expression of the universe, as varied and beautiful as a field of wildflowers, each one a perfect bloom in its own right. Yet, there are moments when the world may make you forget this truth, leading you to believe you need to earn your worth or seek approval from outside yourself.

But your soul, ever patient and faithful, is always there to guide you back. It speaks with a gentle, loving persistence, reminding you that you have nothing to prove. Whether in moments of joy or sorrow, success or perceived failure, you are always enough. Your worth has never been tied to what you do or achieve—it exists simply because you do. You are, and always have been, whole and complete.

The Power of Returning Home

Sweetheart, to return to your divine essence is to set yourself free. It is to step out of the shadows of comparison and let go of the weight of trying to be someone you're not. It is to remember that there is nothing wrong with you—you are not missing, broken, or incomplete.

You are a masterpiece in motion, becoming even more beautiful with every twist and turn of your journey.

In the quiet moments, when you turn inward, you may find parts of yourself that you've tucked away—dreams you thought were too wild, truths you feared were too bold, emotions you believed were too much. But here, in the sanctuary of your soul, those parts are loved unconditionally, just as you are. They belong to you, and they are sacred.

A Reflection of the Universe

My love, think of the stars scattered across the night sky. Each one shines with its own light, adding to the beauty of the cosmos. Just like the stars, you are here not to compete, but simply to shine. You are a part of a grand, cosmic tapestry—a constellation of divinity, unique and irreplaceable.

And just as the moon waxes and wanes, so too do you move through phases—moments of fullness and light, times of retreat and rest. Yet, in every phase, you are whole. The divine essence within you does not falter or fade; it remains steady, always illuminating your path.

An Invitation to Embrace Your Essence

So, my dear one, when life tempts you to prove your worth, pause. Place your hand over your heart, close your eyes, and listen. The quiet wisdom of your soul will always remind you: You are loved. You are whole. You are enough.

Let this moment be a gentle nudge to embrace the truth of who you are. Reflect on a time when you felt the need to prove yourself. Hold that memory with tenderness, and as you do, imagine releasing that need. Feel the weight lift, and instead, lean into the profound truth of your being: You are enough, just as you are.

Let this essay be a soft, melting hug—a mirror reflecting back the light and love that already lives within you. The next time you doubt your worth, let these words wrap around you, reminding you of the sacred flame that burns in your heart.

You are a divine expression of life, my love.
A masterpiece, simply by being.
Never forget that.

How can you cultivate a deeper sense of self-acceptance and self-love, knowing that you carry the whole universe inside of you?

What messages might your soul be trying to send to you right now?

YOU ARE ENOUGH
always
forever

You are free,
within Yourself,
always.

EMOTIONAL SAFETY

I remind myself

It is safe to feel

It is safe to have all these emotions

It is safe to let them out

I am safe within me

I am safe to love me

I am not a burden

I am not a distraction

I am not a fault

I am not a victim

TRUSTING THE SANCTUARY WITHIN

In the gentle embrace of our own hearts lies the sanctuary of emotional safety—a sacred haven where we can unfurl the depths of our emotions without fear or judgment. Yet, in the hustle and bustle of daily life, it is all too easy to lose sight of this inherent refuge within us, forgetting the profound wisdom that resides in the quiet spaces of our being.

Emotional safety is not merely a concept to be understood intellectually; it is a lived experience that calls for our conscious presence and attention. It beckons us to return home to ourselves, to cultivate a deep sense of trust in the inherent goodness and resilience of our hearts.

When we remind ourselves that it is safe to feel, we are affirming our innate capacity to navigate the rich tapestry of human emotions—both light and shadow, joy and sorrow, love and fear. We are acknowledging that each emotion, no matter how uncomfortable or challenging, is a precious gift, offering us valuable insights into our inner landscape and guiding us toward greater self-awareness and healing.

In the quiet moments of reflection, we come to realize that emotional safety is not something to be found outside of ourselves but rather a sacred birthright that resides within the depths of our being. It is not something we must earn or prove; it is already ours, waiting patiently for us to remember.

A Trust Fall Into Our Soul

Creating emotional safety is like a trust fall in the arms of our own soul. It asks us to surrender to the wisdom and guidance that emanate from the core of our being. In this sanctuary, we find the courage to sit with our emotions, even the ones we have labeled as "too much" or "too painful." It is here, within this sacred space, that we begin to soften, allowing ourselves to be fully seen and held in all our messy, imperfect glory.

But trusting this sanctuary within requires both courage and vulnerability. It calls us to confront the stories we've been told—the ones that whisper we are unworthy or undeserving of love and acceptance. These stories, though loud at times, are not the truth of who we are. They are shadows cast by fear, and like all shadows, they fade when we bring them into the light.

Releasing the armor we've built around our hearts is not an easy task. It can feel like stepping into the unknown, peeling back layers of protection we've held onto for so long. But, my dear one, it is in this release that we discover the strength and resilience of our own hearts—the unwavering light that shines within us, even amidst life's storms.

The Beauty of Feeling Safe to Feel

When we create a sanctuary within ourselves, we gift our emotions the space they need to flow freely. We allow joy to dance, sorrow to speak, and fear to soften. This is the beauty of feeling safe to feel. Our emotions are no longer something to be managed or suppressed but sacred messengers guiding us ever deeper into the heart of our own humanity.

In this safety, we come to understand that we are not our emotions. They do not define us; they move through us. Like waves on the shore, they rise and fall, but the ocean of our being remains steady and infinite.

An Invitation to Trust Yourself

Sweetheart, let us remind ourselves that we are not burdens, distractions, faults, or victims. We are divine beings, capable of navigating the ebbs and flows of life with grace and resilience.

You are worthy of love and acceptance, just as you are, in this moment.

Take a deep breath, and with it, remind yourself:

It is safe to feel. It is safe to cry, to laugh, to grieve, to hope, to love. Your emotions are not here to harm you—they are here to teach you, to guide you, to reveal the depths of your strength and the tenderness of your soul.

Let my words serve as a gentle nudge back to the sanctuary within you. Picture your heart as a sacred space, warm and inviting, where all parts of you are welcome. Wrap yourself in its embrace and know that no matter what life brings, you carry this haven within you, always.

You are safe here, my love.
You are whole.
You are enough.

How does your heartspace look when you build your sanctuary of safety in it?

In what ways can you show yourself compassion and kindness when faced with challenging emotions?

How can you create a safe space for yourself to feel and process your emotions?

CYCLE & SEASONS

The Rhythm of Life

Life moves in rhythms, much like the changing seasons that cradle the earth. Within each of us, there lies a quiet echo of this ancient dance—a sacred reminder that we, too, are part of nature's endless cycles. Just as winter gives way to the blossoms of spring, and the warmth of summer yields to autumn's gentle release, so do we evolve, grow, release, and renew.

The cycles we move through are not mere coincidences; they are invitations to align with the natural rhythm of life, to honor the ebb and flow within ourselves. Each phase holds its own wisdom, its own unique gift to guide us closer to our true essence.

Honoring Your Inner Seasons

My love, it's important to remember: that there is no one "right" way to move through life's seasons.

Just as every flower blooms in its own time, and every tree finds its unique rhythm to flourish, so do you carry your own pace, your own sacred dance.

It's okay if your winter feels longer, your spring takes time to bloom, or if you're still shedding leaves while others are basking in the light of their summer. The rhythm of your life is a song only you can sing, and the wisdom of your soul knows exactly when to grow, when to rest, and when to release. Trust this inner wisdom—it is guiding you with the same grace that moves the tides and shifts the stars.

The Gift of Surrender

Some seasons will call you to let go, to release what no longer serves you, like trees surrendering their golden leaves to the wind. Others will ask you to rest, to embrace stillness as a sacred act of nurturing, trusting that beneath the surface, life is quietly unfolding.

And then, there will be moments of blossoming, when the dreams you've held in the fertile soil of your soul begin to take form. Each phase, whether marked by growth or release, is a vital part of your journey—a reminder that endings are not failures but beginnings in disguise.

An Invitation to Reflection

This section invites you to embrace the beauty in your own cycles and to see the sacred purpose in every phase of your journey. Let it be a gentle reminder that every ending is a beginning, and that surrender creates space for something new to take root.

May you find comfort in knowing that you are always held by the rhythm of life and that within every season, there is a gift waiting to be discovered.

A MESSAGE FROM GAIA AND LUNA

Beloved Child of the Earth and Sky,

We speak to you as one, our voices intertwined like the ancient dance of creation. We are Gaia, the ground beneath your feet, and Luna, the light that softly illuminates your nights. Together, we remind you of the cycles that cradle your life, the sacred rhythm that mirrors the ebb and flow of your very breath.

From Gaia, I whisper: Remember the soil that births new life after the fall of leaves, the roots that grow strongest in the darkness of the earth. I hold you as you shed what no longer serves you, offering you the courage to bloom anew when your time comes. Trust the seasons of your soul as deeply as you trust the arrival of spring after winter's stillness.

From Luna, I murmur: Remember the tides I pull, the rhythm of rise and retreat that mirrors the energy within you. My light waxes and wanes, reminding you that even in your moments of rest or retreat, you are whole. Let my phases teach you the power of honoring your cycles, knowing that the time for radiance and renewal will always return.

Together, we remind you that you carry us within you. The dust of stars and moons flows in your veins, while the soil of Gaia grounds your every step. You are the child of both earth and sky, a living embodiment of harmony between light and shadow, stillness and motion.

So, dear one, do not rush your seasons. Do not fear your own tides. Let yourself surrender to the natural rhythm that flows through your being. In every phase, you are held. In every season, you are loved.

With every breath, feel our essence within you—stable, cyclical, eternal. We are here, always.

With endless love and guidance,

Gaia and Luna

The Earth is You

I AM THE SEASONS

I am the Seasons
every changing
but always
myself

EMBRACING THE SEASONS WITHIN

Just as the earth cycles through her seasons, so do we flow through phases of growth, release, and renewal. There is a quiet beauty in this rhythm—a reminder that change is not something to resist but something to embrace as part of our human journey.

Like the seasons, we are constantly in flux. There are times when we feel like the vibrant bloom of spring, alive with possibility and bursting with new energy. Then, there are the days of summer, when we bask in the fullness of our purpose, radiating confidence and vitality. Inevitably, autumn arrives, inviting us to shed what no longer serves us, like golden leaves falling to the earth. And winter—oh, winter, with its quiet stillness—asks us to rest, to reflect, and to gather strength for the new beginnings to come.

Honoring Your Inner Cycles

My love, your journey is as unique as a tree standing strong through the changing seasons. While one tree blooms early in spring, another waits for its own perfect time. So it is with you—there is no right way, no singular rhythm that you must follow. Your inner seasons unfold in their own sacred timing, and this timing is yours to honor.

Yes, I know I am repeating myself, but this is a truth worth repeating: your inner seasons are sacred. They are not meant to mirror anyone else's journey. This is your path, your rhythm, your unfolding. Trust in it, my love, even if it looks different from what the world might expect. There is wisdom in your rhythm, a knowing that flows from the depths of your soul.

You may find yourself in winter while others are in summer, or in the shedding of autumn while someone else is bursting with spring energy. And that's okay. Each phase carries its own beauty, its own lessons. Trust that your pace is perfect, just as it is.

The Essence That Remains

Amidst all this change, there is a core within you that remains unshaken—your eternal essence, the "always myself" that grounds you no matter the season. This essence is your anchor, your constant amidst the ebb and flow. It reminds you that even in the middle of transitions, you are whole, complete, and enough, just as you are.

An Invitation to Reflect

As you embrace the seasons within you, take a moment to pause and honor the gifts of each phase: the fresh energy of spring, the vibrant power of summer, the quiet wisdom of autumn, and the restorative stillness of winter. Each season holds something sacred for you to discover, something to guide you back to yourself.

My love, remember that you are a cyclic being, living on a cyclic planet. Each season, both within and around you, is a gift to be celebrated and cherished. Trust in your rhythm, for it is as timeless and sacred as the cycles of the earth herself.

Imagine yourself as a tree, deeply rooted in the earth, experiencing the changing seasons.

How do you stay grounded and steady amidst life's inevitable changes?

Take a moment to connect with the energy of each season within yourself.

How can you align with the natural rhythms of the earth to integrate and increase a deeper sense of harmony and balance in your life?

Beauty is within You

UNFOLDING

I am unfolding like a rose

Layer by layer

Petal by petal

At my own pace

I reveal my wholeness

I embrace my beauty

I embody my growth

I surrender into my transformation

I am unfolding like a rose

UNFOLDING INTO WHOLENESS

The Rhythm of Unfolding

In the delicate dance of life, we often find ourselves unfolding, much like a rose opening its petals to the world. Each layer peeled back reveals a deeper aspect of ourselves, a facet of our being waiting to be embraced and celebrated.

The rose reminds us to trust the process of unfolding and to allow ourselves to reveal our wholeness, beauty, and growth at our own pace. It invites us to surrender into the transformational journey of life here on earth, trusting in the inherent wisdom of our souls to guide us along the way.

Trusting the Timing

There is no need to rush this sacred process. Just as a rose cannot be forced to bloom before its time, we, too, cannot pull back our layers prematurely. Aggressively opening the flower disrupts its natural rhythm, robbing it of its grace. Each petal knows when to unfurl; each layer reveals itself in its own perfect timing.

You are not in a race to transform. The rose blooms not by looking to others, but by listening to its own rhythm, trusting the sunlight and rain to nurture it when the moment is right. So, too, should you honor the timing of your own unfolding. Trust that everything within you will bloom when it is meant to, guided by the wisdom that already resides in your soul.

The Liberation of Growth

Like a rose in bloom, we are in a constant state of growth and evolution. With each layer shed, we come closer to embodying our true essence and embracing the fullness of who we are. This journey is not without moments of vulnerability, for it asks us to step into the unknown, to release what no longer serves us. But in this vulnerability, we find courage. And in this courage, we discover the profound beauty of our becoming.

In the act of unfolding, we release the constraints of self-doubt and limitation, allowing ourselves to expand into the fullness of our being. We embrace our unique beauty and inherent worthiness, recognizing that we are worthy of love and acceptance exactly as we are.

The rose reminds us that boundaries, too, are sacred. She stands tall in her Queendom, her thorns a gentle yet firm declaration of what is hers to protect. In her unfolding, she teaches us that blooming does not mean sacrificing our safety. It means honoring what is sacred within us and setting boundaries that nurture our growth.

An Invitation to Reflect

So, my lovely roses, I invite you to take a moment to reflect on the rose unfolding within you. Consider the layers you have yet to peel back, the aspects of yourself waiting to be revealed, or the boundaries that need tending. Trust in the wisdom of your soul, and allow yourself to embrace this journey with an open heart and mind.

Know that you are a beautiful work in progress—a masterpiece in the making. Embrace your growth, celebrate your beauty, and surrender into the transformative power of your own unfolding.

My love, take a moment to honor the courage it takes to unfold like a rose—layer by layer, petal by petal, trusting in the natural rhythm of your being.

How can you honor the timing of your unfolding, trusting that each layer will reveal itself when it is ready?

What boundaries can you set to protect your growth and nurture your transformation?

How does it feel to embrace your own beauty and embody the courage it takes to bloom fully?

My Love,
You are Nature

NATURE'S DAUGHTER

She loves the ocean

as she was birthed by sirens

She whispers to the moon

as she was raised by wolves

She prayed to Mother Earth

because she is her child

THE WILD WITHIN CONNECTION AND BELONGING

The Untamed Heart

There lives an untamed wilderness in every soul—a sacred realm where mystery and magic dance together in perfect harmony. It is a place where the boundaries between the human and the divine dissolve, where ancient whispers echo through the corridors of time, calling us back to the truth of who we are:

Wild. Untethered. Infinitely free.

This wilderness is not something to fear but something to embrace—a reminder of the wild ones we once were and the wildness that still lives within us. Each heartbeat invites us to step deeper into the untamed spaces of our souls, to reconnect with the primal forces that shape our existence and guide us back to our essence.

A Longing for Connection

Within this wildness lies a profound longing—a desire to return to the elemental energies that course through the veins of the earth and stars. This is the longing for connection, for belonging, for the raw, unfiltered truth of who we are.

Like the ocean, we are fluid and ever-changing, ebbing and flowing with the tides of life. We are birthed from its depths, cradled by sirens who sing ancient lullabies of longing and desire. Their voices call us to dive deep into the waters of our own souls, to uncover the treasures hidden beneath the surface.

Like the moon, we are luminous and mysterious, casting our light upon the darkness. We are raised by wolves who teach us instinct and intuition, guiding us along the path of our inner knowing. Their howls pierce the silence, reminding us of the primal wisdom etched into our very bones.

And above all, we are children of Mother Earth. She is our sacred source, the nurturer who sustains and holds us in her loving arms. In her embrace, we find sanctuary—a place to lay our burdens and remember that we are loved beyond measure.

Honoring the Wild Within

My love, let us follow the call of the wild. Let us embrace the untamed beauty within us and honor the sacred connection that binds us to Mother Earth and the stars. For in the wildness of our souls, we find our truest expression:

> ***Beings of light and love,***
> ***dancing in the eternal rhythm of creation.***

When did you last howl at the moon? Never? Oh, my dear, it's time to untame your wild side. Howl, scream, sing under the moonlight. Feel the primal energy of your wild heart beating in your chest. Use your voice—your unique siren song. It is your most powerful magnet, calling forth your desires and dreams into reality.

Run barefoot through the mud, jump into a puddle, and laugh until your sides ache. Untaming the child within you, the carefree version of yourself who is unburdened by the world's judgments. Let the whispers of the sirens and the wisdom of the wolves remind you that life is not meant to be tamed—it is meant to be lived.

This is your invitation to reconnect with the wilderness of your being, to feel the primal energies that have guided you across lifetimes. Trust in your resilience, your strength, and your grace. Honor the wild within you, for it is the heartbeat of your soul and the bridge to the universe itself.

Connect with the wild and untamed essence of your soul

How can you honor and embrace your unique essence, allowing it to guide you on your path?

In what ways can you deepen your connection to the elemental forces of nature, finding strength in their wisdom and grace?

How does it feel to surrender to the wild rhythm of your soul, trusting its untamed beauty to lead you?

NECTAR OF LIFE

I want to taste every drop
of the nectar of my holy life,
to savor the sweetness
and the bitterness,
to let each season of my existence
flow through me,
unfolding like petals beneath the sun
and the moon,
dancing with the quiet whispers of time,
to feel every pulse of the earth within my veins,
to drink deeply from the well
of my own becoming
I want the nectar of life
dripping from my tongue

SAVOR THE NECTAR OF LIFE

The Alchemy of Existence

There is a sacred alchemy in the dance between light and shadow, a quiet unfolding that invites us to taste the fullness of our existence. Life, in its essence, is not a journey to be rushed or merely endured; it is a sacred ritual, an intimate dance with the divine essence within and around us.

Every moment, like a droplet of nectar, holds the essence of the universe. It is both fleeting and eternal, delicate yet profound. This nectar, a metaphor for the richness of our experiences, urges us to taste deeply—to relish the sweetness of joy, the sharp tang of sorrow, the bittersweet flavor of transitions. It is through this tasting that we come to know ourselves, not just as beings of light but as creatures woven with shadow, with layers that reflect the rhythm of the cosmos.

Savoring Life's Rhythms

To savor the nectar of life is to honor the seasons within us—the times of blooming and the periods of quiet dormancy, the vibrant summers of expansion, and the reflective winters of rest. Each phase carries its own beauty, its own lesson, and its own gift. Yes, my darlings, I'm repeating, we all need to be reminded about how sacred our very own seasons are.

There is no rush in this sacred unfolding. Like the Maiden, we are not here to sprint through the chapters of our lives but to savor them, to be touched and transformed by each page. Life invites us to slow down, to notice the delicate details: the way sunlight filters through autumn leaves, the sound of rain against a window, the tender embrace of solitude.

Each moment is a droplet of nectar, a whisper from the universe reminding us that we are not just observers but participants in a grand, cosmic dance.

Embracing Wholeness

In embracing the nectar of life, we also embrace our wholeness. We honor the vast tapestry of our experiences, understanding that every drop—whether sweet or bitter—is essential to the story of our soul. To savor life is to deepen our connection to the cycles of nature, to the unseen threads that bind us to the cosmos, and to the sacred rhythm of our own becoming.

The Maiden archetype reminds us to delight in life's richness, to see beauty in every moment, and to embrace the grace that exists in simply being. When we pause to taste the nectar of life, we are reminded that we are not separate from this world—we are the world, woven into its sacred rhythms.

How can you savor the sweetness of this moment, allowing yourself to pause and truly feel its beauty?

What "bitter" drops in your life might hold a hidden gift, waiting to be discovered with time?

How can you embody the energy of the Maiden, celebrating life with curiosity, wonder, and presence?

When was the last time you let yourself truly slow down, to notice the details, to savor the nectar of your own existence?

You Are Found

You Are Whole

GRATITUDE

To all the luminous souls who hold this book in their hands: **Thank you**. Thank you for trusting my creations, for allowing my words to touch your heart, and for walking this sacred journey alongside me. Your support means more than words could ever express—you are part of the magic that brought this book to life.

My deepest gratitude flows to the souls who walk beside me, seen and unseen. To my Lioness Queen, Michaela, who is the embodiment of courage and grace, always reminding me to trust my path and roar with my truth. Your encouragement is a light that has guided me through the dark.

To the universe, the unseen forces, and the energies that cradle me in their tender embrace: Thank you. To my Spirit Guide and beloved Ancestors, who whisper wisdom and courage into my soul: Thank you for walking this path with me, for holding me steady, and for teaching me how to rise.

And to the one who sees me, loves me, and calls me "my Luna baby girl"—your love is the quiet flame that keeps my heart warm. You are my anchor, my safe haven, and my greatest gift. My love and gratitude are yours, endlessly.

And lastly, I turn my gratitude inward, to myself. Thank you, Ophelia, for walking this sacred path with courage and devotion. For every moment you've crumbled, only to rise again—stronger, wiser, and more radiant than before. Thank you for embracing the shadows, for surrendering to the unknown, and for daring to dream boldly. You are the foundation of this creation, and you deserve all the love and praise you so freely give to others.

From the depths of my soul, thank YOU. You are a part of this creation, and for that, I will always hold you close in my heart.

ABOUT THE AUTHOR

Ophelia Amaru is a soulful seeker, intuitive healer, and poetic weaver of light. As an author and guide, she is devoted to illuminating the sacred path of self-discovery and inner transformation for women. With a heart that beats to the rhythm of the cosmos and a spirit that flows like water, Ophelia's words are a gentle, yet profound invitation to come home to yourself.

Born from the ashes of her own healing and spiritual awakening, Ophelia's creations—her poems, prayers, meditations, and sacred offerings—are a tender embrace for the soul. She writes not only to inspire but to guide you to explore the depths of your being, reconnect with your divine essence, and awaken the sacred feminine energy within.

Through her deeply intuitive work, Ophelia weaves the energy of love and compassion into every word, offering a sanctuary where you are invited to reclaim your power, honor your whole-

ness, and step fully into the light of your true self. Her creations are infused with the wisdom of the divine feminine, the stillness of the moonlit night, and the grounding essence of the earth—reminding you of your infinite potential and your sa-  *cred connection to the universe.*

Ophelia's work is an ode to the transformative power of living a soul-led life. She believes in the beauty of imperfection, the strength found in vulnerability, and the profound magic of simply being. Her journey, and the heartfelt creations born from it, are an offering to you—a beacon of light, a safe harbor in the chaos, and an invitation to embrace the sacred within yourself.

May you always remember:
You are whole. You are divine. You are sacred.

SOUL CONNECTION

Dearest Souls,

It fills my heart with so much joy to connect with you, wherever you are in this world. I believe that stories, art, and heartfelt connections weave the threads that bind us together. Your voice, your thoughts, your creations—they matter deeply to me.

✶ *Let's Connect* ✶

I would love to hear what resonates with you. Share your reflections, your favorite lines, or simply drop a note to say hello. I welcome your messages with an open heart:

Instagram: @ophelia.amaru

Website: ophelia-amaru.com

Email: sacred-souls@ophelia-amaru.com

☽ *A Personal Touch* ☾

I have dreamed of a way to give back to this beautiful community, and you—my cherished readers. Imagine receiving a handwritten note, a keepsake made just for you, arriving in your mailbox, no matter where you are on this planet.

Doesn't it feel a little nostalgic, like stepping back into the magic of the 90s? Sending letters and postcards—something tangible, infused with love and care. I would be honored to create something uniquely for you, to bridge the pages of this book with the connection of a handwritten touch.

Here's how you can receive yours:

Take a picture of my book in your favorite space, or capture a snippet of a poem, prayer, or passage that speaks to your soul.

Share it on Instagram and tag me: @ophelia.amaru

Not on Instagram? No problem! Send your picture via email to:
sacred-souls@ophelia-amaru.com

With each note I write, I wish to remind you of how deeply you are loved, how connected we are, and how powerful your light truly is.

Don't forget to message me your address.

With all my love,

Ophelia Amaru

MY GIFT FOR YOU

(completely FREE)

As a heartfelt thank you for holding this book in your hands, I've created a guided meditation to help you tap into your cosmic energy and reconnect with your celestial essence.

✶ Guided Meditation ✶
"Remembering Your Celestial Essence"

This meditation is my gift to you—a gentle invitation to remember the truth of who you are:
infinite, radiant, and made of stardust.

✶ How to Access:

Scan the QR code

Visit my Instagram Highlights "Offerings"
@ophelia.amaru

Or simply visit:
https://ophelia-amaru.com/celestial-essence

OFFERINGS

Beyond the pages of this book, I'm honored to create spaces and offerings that nurture your journey of self-discovery and healing.

✶ Monthly Online Ceremony ✶

A sacred space hosted in both German & English. Choose your language and join me for a ceremony to honor your inner journey.
Donation Based

ophelia-amaru.com/ceremonies

✶ Meditation Sanctuary ✶
"Wholeness Within"

A pre-recorded meditation bundle designed to guide you deeper into the spaces between the words and the whispers of your soul.
Available March 2025 - you'll find updates on my Instagram and my Website.

✶ And So Much More to Come ✶

Stay tuned, as I continue to weave magic into new creations to support and inspire your sacred path. Follow me on Instagram to stay tuned and connected.
@ophelia.amaru

EXCLUSIVE READER GIFT

As one of my beloved readers, you're invited to enjoy 10% off all my offerings—now and in the future, anytime!

Use Code: **SoulContact**

With all my love and blessings,

Ophelia

Space for Reflection & Dreams

www.ingramcontent.com/pod-product-compliance
Ingram Content Group UK Ltd.
Pitfield, Milton Keynes, MK11 3LW, UK
UKHW040708060526
12295UKWH00011B/93